P9-DMG-565

# ELTON JOHN'S

## FLOWER FANTASIES

# ELTON JOHN'S
# FLOWER
# FANTASIES

**An Intimate Tour of His Houses and Garden**

**Caroline Cass**

Flowers by
**Julia Wigan**
and **Susan Hill**

Photography by
**Andrew Twort**

A BULFINCH PRESS BOOK
LITTLE, BROWN AND COMPANY
BOSTON•NEW YORK•TORONTO•LONDON

Text copyright © 1997 by Caroline Cass

Photographs copyright © 1997 by Andrew Twort

Compilation and layout copyright © 1997 by George Weidenfeld & Nicolson Ltd

All rights reserved. No part of this book may be reproduced in any form or by any electronic or mechanical means, including information storage and retrieval
systems, without permission in writing from the publisher, except by a reviewer
who may quote brief passages in a review.

First published in Great Britain 1997
by George Weidenfeld & Nicolson Ltd
The Orion Publishing Group
5 Upper St. Martin's Lane
London WC2H 9EA

First United States Edition

ISBN 0-8212-2467-0

Library of Congress Catalog Card Number 97-71947

Bulfinch Press is an imprint and trademark of Little, Brown and Company (Inc.)

PRINTED IN ITALY

## FOR ELTON

*' It could be said of me that in this book
I have only made up a bunch of other
men's flowers, providing of my own
only the string that ties them together. '*

MICHEL DE MONTAIGNE (1533 – 92)

# $\mathcal{C}$ontents

# Introduction

*So out of choice I chose rock 'n' roll*
*But it pushed me to the limit every day,*
*It turned me into a gypsy, kept me away from home...*

'BETWEEN SEVENTEEN AND TWENTY', music by Elton John, lyrics by Taupin.

The simple flower is a powerful and enduring symbol of both beauty and romance. Elton John, the legendary and greatly loved superstar, has a passion for nature's most delicate creation – a craving not usually associated with rock icons. Rockers and roses, pop and peonies, would appear odd bedfellows – once upon a time most self-respecting rockstars revelled in the lowlife. But Elton has always marched to a different drum. He started young by winning a scholarship to the Royal Academy of Music in London aged eleven, a feat achieved by none of his peers.

Apart from the leviathan Elvis Presley, Elton is the biggest solo artist in rock music's history. For over a quarter of a century he has woven a labyrinthine web of images in his songs, and he still is to rock lovers what Andy Warhol was to pop counterculture – a contemporary cult icon. People care about Elton; he matters to them. His appeal is universal, embracing adolescents to oldies, and his name belongs to the small circle of greats who have made an indelible impact on us – the Beatles, the Rolling Stones, Eric Clapton, Bob Dylan and Presley.

Having risen to fame as a singer and songwriter, an enduring recording artist, and a flamboyant stage performer who pounded the keys in outrageous costumes – once playing to five hundred thousand people in Central Park while dressed as Donald Duck – Elton became a spender on a heroic scale. Although known to be a sensitive and stylish man, a discerning connoisseur and art collector, as well as maintaining a keen interest in design and decoration, indulging his weakness for flowers remains a largely private affair and one unknown to his legions of admirers. At home he is surrounded daily by fresh flowers, a cat's cradle of blossoms which weave a constant symmetry throughout every room in 'Captain Fantastic's' two houses in London and Old Windsor.

The life and times of Elton have undergone an astonishing metamorphosis. His vast collection of Art Nouveau and Art Deco artefacts has been sold. His destructive and often tumultuous history is behind him, and he has recently drawn a line through his past by celebrating six years of abstinence from alcohol and drugs. After twenty-five years at the top, Elton has emerged as a true survivor. Nowadays, the former hellraiser relies on calm and ordered surroundings filled with antiques and objects of intrinsic charm to soothe away the excesses of a peripatetic life on the road. His love of flowers is simply an extension of his empathy with all things beautiful. 'I never gave myself time to stop and smell the roses. Well, now I can stop and I'm going to. I just want to smell a few roses', Elton once said.

He is inordinately proud of his houses. 'Elton's house is a symbol of his transformation and his current happiness', says David Furnish, his partner for the past four years. And so it would seem. Amid a relaxed atmosphere, sunny pools of flowers sparkle in both his rambling, rosy-coloured Queen Anne-style house in the country and his London home. With a happy and settled personal life, perhaps it is when he is endeavouring to lead a normal life, surrounded by his beloved dogs, his treasured possessions and his flowers and gardens, that Elton finds his greatest measure of contentment. Despite, or perhaps precisely because of his fame, Elton would appear an ideal advocate of John Ruskin's statement: 'Flowers seem intended for the solace of ordinary humanity.'

Most civilizations have loved and cultivated flowers – like a thread of colour woven into the tapestry of our lives, flowers and plants are inextricably bound up with mankind's survival. Although many of us no longer live in close harmony with nature, and as wild flowers become increasingly rare and rainforests disappear, there can be few people who do not take a delight in flowering plants. The English, in particular, have always been recognized for their obsession with gardening and their respect for nature's inherent splendour. With their myriad colours, evocative scents, variety of shapes and textures, the natural beauty of flowers touches a number of senses at once – the silky translucency of a shell-pink rose; the delicate scent of lilacs. They instantly transform our surroundings, fixing for a brief time an image of decorative grace and giving us a renewed sense of tranquility. Flowers satisfy our instinctive need for a more gentle world by evoking the unattainable dream world of our childhood, where all was simplicity and innocence. They also provide us with a touch of romance . Given Elton's prodigious sense of theatre, what could be more romantic than Cleopatra welcoming her lover, Mark Anthony, into a room strewn with the petals of ten thousand roses, or sprinkling the sails of her ship with perfumed rose-water as she sailed down the Nile, so that 'the very winds were love-sick'?

At its most inspired, flower-arranging is one of the great arts, representing the essence of a cultural tradition possibly best depicted in the flower paintings of the seventeenth-century Dutch masters. When I suggested a book celebrating the flowers in his houses and gardens to him, Elton enthusiastically agreed, as long as 'the book is beautiful and not gimmicky' – as always a discerning élan is of the utmost importance to him. With the invaluable help and creative abilities of my sister, Susie Hill, and her partner, Julia Wigan, of Bloomingdale Flowers, who complete up to 240 flower arrangements each week for Elton, and without whom this book would not have been possible, as well as Andrew Twort's sensitive photography and imaginative ideas, I have tried my best to comply.

CAROLINE CASS

The fabled Elton spectacles are copied in flowers – a profusion of red carnations, canary-yellow chrysanthemums, blue hydrangeas, deep mauve anemones and orange marigolds.

# Red & Orange

For every rose he gives her I'll give her three
But in the meantime I'll just wish that he was me.

'I FALL APART' – MUSIC BY ELTON JOHN, LYRICS BY TAUPIN.

*Spring is my favourite season. My most perfect day would be
a spring day with the first sprinkling of green in the garden,
the buds flowering on the trees and daffodils lining the
driveway. In May, I love walking in my woods and looking
at the sea of bluebells.*

ELTON JOHN

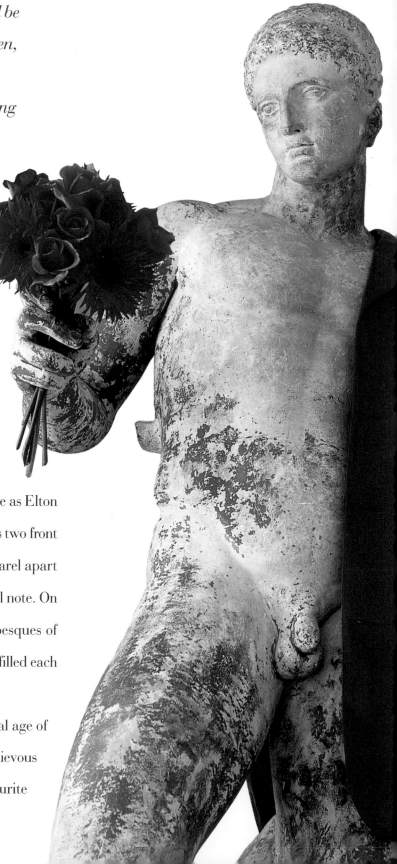

*I*t was a cool English summer morning when
Elton first talked at length about his love of flowers at Woodside, his
country house near Windsor. The smell of newly mown lawns and
scented honeysuckle hung lightly in the air. Bees, busily discussing
their choice of flowers for the day, buzzed lazily around the entrance as Elton
greeted me with a smile as prominent as the famous gap between his two front
teeth. A fluffy white towelling robe and loafers – his favourite apparel apart
from tracksuits when lounging at home – struck a suitably informal note. On
our way to the drawing room groups of flowers cut elegant arabesques of
pattern, giving warmth and colour to the house. Their heady scent filled each
room.

Elton appeared relaxed and seemed more boyish than his actual age of
forty-nine years. His is an appealing face, reminding one of a mischievous
child who has just been caught dressing up in his mother's favourite

*An imposing figure of a young man nonchalantly flings the jacket of Elton's favourite tomato-red PVC suit over his shoulder. The suit is one that Elton frequently wears at his concerts. For many years the nineteenth-century statue, after Canova, resided over the original Carlsberg Brewery's factory gates in Copenhagen. In his new home he proffers a simple bunch of 'Chamilla' and 'Jacaranda' roses combined with the florist's new dream flower, the spiky gerbera 'Doctor Who'.*

*Roses are always placed in Elton's bedroom because he loves them. The talented furniture designer David Linley (the nephew of Queen Elizabeth II) has designed the façade of a three-storey Palladian mansion in parquetry to cover the walls surrounding Elton's bed. A Versace dressing gown is flung across Elton's sheets. In front of the luscious cluster of fully-opened roses lies a diamond-and-ruby Cartier watch, while behind the arrangement sit silver-framed photographs of Elton and his friends. The large lion in the picture with Elton was from the Disney Studios for the promotion of* The Lion King, *which featured songs by Elton and Tim Rice.*

*Elton's interior designers were sent to Milan to see his friend Gianni Versace's bath to gain inspiration for the construction of his own. The only similarity is the classical concept. A pair of embroidered slippers touch Elton's silk vermillion Versace dressing gown. The dominant feature on the marble bath is the sculpture of a bronze lion's-head mask from which the water pours. Complementing the colours of the gown is a dramatic arrangement of scarlet ginger stems mixed with dark-cerise antirrhinum, gerbera 'lynx', lilac-coloured delphinium, blue lisianthus and branches of rosehip. Behind can be seen a large study after the antique Apollo Belvedere by Charles Landseer .*

evening gown. Little escapes the scrutiny of his hazel-brown, seen-it-all eyes. His lack of a full head of hair, for many years a distressing factor in his life, is now a shining, auburn-brown mop, thanks to a weave. Baby fine, it falls neatly forward from the crown of his head and spills over his bushy eyebrows, brushing the rim of a pair of his famed gold spectacles.

During our discussion, Elton oscillated between effortless charm and thoughtful introspection. His candour, evident confidence and jaunty disrespect when talking about himself can only be a refreshing substitute for the days when he was plugged into the dubious pleasures of alcohol and cocaine. He spoke in an accentless voice and was articulate, sharp-witted, and full of enthusiasm about his homes, gardens, flowers, diverse interests and David, his partner. Having previously been asked what he most enjoyed about his lover, David's comment that Elton knew the short cut to his funny bone immediately sprang to mind: 'He makes me laugh. He's funny and very witty and whenever I'm around him I find myself cracking up with laughter.' An easy shyness; no obvious whiff of rebellion these days for a man who appears totally without conceit.

It transpired that for Elton flowers primarily symbolize the eternal cycle and soothing rhythms of nature.

*I really care about the seasons and watching things grow. After all, flowers and plants are such an integral part of human life. In the house where I was born, in Pinner Hill Road, we had a beautiful garden and we always had a mass of flowers in the house throughout my childhood. Even though the gardens of my youth were small and suburban, they were invariably pretty.*

Elton enjoys the same celebration of renewal and hope that most of us feel when the first signs of spring appear with its offering of snowdrops – 'February fairmaids' – and crocuses.

*Here I can't wait to see the tulips, daffodils and camellias, in the glade down by the ornamental lake, come out. At my home in Atlanta, Georgia, I look forward to the petals of the magnolia tree, which have a lovely texture of thick cream, unfolding, as well as the dogwood flowers and azaleas. All the trees and shrubs in Georgia seem to bloom at once, so spring in both places is wonderful.*

His is the universal ritual of impatience following the long winter months when the dormant secrets of the garden are hidden by a brown blanket of earth; when bare trees remain the colour of bone. However inclement the weather and however inconsiderate people may be to the living world around them, the seasons try never to fail us in their loyalty. Year after year familiar flowers return. We can rely on ribbons of yellow daffodils rippling in the spring breeze, just as we can look forward to woodland bluebells in May, 'as if a blue cloud had fallen from the face of heaven, lighting up the darkness of the forest'.

'Flowers sparkled in my childhood as they do in a medieval manuscript', Derek Jarman, the film-maker and writer wrote not long before he died. Similarly, Elton's earliest memory of flowers centres round his childhood garden.

*Sir Roy Strong, the eminent former head of the Victoria and Albert Museum and the foremost expert on Tudor England – now turned garden designer – was commissioned to create an Italian garden outside the drawing room. Four stone statues of musicians stand proudly in the midst of fiery-scarlet geraniums and boxwood circles. A graceful blend of Tuscan-yellow ochre and soft-grey Italianate pavilions, urns, benches and balustrades, all of which were specially made in Italy, complete the Mediterranean ambience.*

*It's a little bit funny this feeling inside I'm not one of those that can easily hide I don't have much money but boy if I did I'd buy a big house where we both could live*

'MONA LISA AND MAD HATTERS'

MUSIC BY ELTON JOHN, LYRICS BY TAUPIN.

*My grandfather died when I was five and my grandmother, Ivy, eventually remarried a man called Horace Sewell who had one leg – he had lost the other in the First World War. He was the first person I knew who was crazy about gardening. He worked for a gardening firm in Pinner and was a most amazing gardener – a real dahlia man. Besides our garden, which he loved, Horace had a couple of allotments and he grew the most incredible flowers – roses; his beloved dahlias which he used to exhibit at the local agricultural show every year; chrysanthemums, which I don't particularly care for; sweet peas and various vegetables. To be fair, my grandmother Ivy always loved gardening too and was a marvellous gardener. So they were both extremely influential.*

The smells of childhood hold eternal, poignant memories – the smell of the earth after rain; fortresses of autumn leaves burning on a bonfire at the stolen hour of twilight; foraging rambles through scented meadows which often turn into voyages of discovery. As a child Elton remembers the ephemeral presence of certain flowers giving him particular pleasure.

*Besides roses – my favourite flower – I have always loved antirrhinums [snapdragons], and the 'dreaded', old-fashioned wallflowers – the flower of love in adversity – which I think are so pretty. And since childhood I have adored dahlias, asters and stocks.*

*An ornate pair of console tables in the Orangery's drawing room were based on an eighteenth-century, early baroque, carved and giltwood pair designed by William Kent which reside at Houghton Hall, the seat of Lord Cholmondeley in Norfolk. Two fine, nineteenth-century, turquoise-enamel and gilt urns add their delicate colour to that of a Regency candelabra, which stretches up as if to touch the gilded shell at the top of the elaborate mirror. Seemingly holding up the table, a chubby cherub sits on a scallop shell. Both mirrors and tables took Elton's cabinet-maker over six months to complete. The portrait of the effeminate Count de Ruppelmonde (1707), decked out in armour and peruke, which is one of a pair by Nicolas de Largillière, hangs on the wall leading to the small library. A spray of blood-red 'Royal Velvet' amaryllis lies on a French, eighteenth-century chair covered in grey-green Fortuny silk.*

# Culivate the freshest flower
## This garden ever grew.

'CURTAINS' –
MUSIC BY ELTON JOHN,
LYRICS BY TAUPIN.

Being an introverted young boy, Elton spent hours playing alone in the garden among his grandparents' dew-laden roses and prize blooms. Besides the colour, it is often the shape of a flower which arouses a child's interest, particularly those with the shape of a bell. Elton can still recall the fragile, lavender-blue Canterbury bell, so called because it resembled the tinkling bells which Chaucer's pilgrims used for decorating their horses' harnesses on their ride to St Thomas à Becket's shrine. And how much easier for a small person to understand Vita Sackville-West's view that 'The flowers I like best

*Elton's Oscar takes a bow on stage. Heavy floral curtains featuring red chrysanthemums are parted to reveal the glittering gold statue, standing proudly against a backdrop of blush-peach 'Romey' roses. Inscribed on the Oscar's base are the following words:*

ACADEMY AWARD
TO
'CAN YOU FEEL THE LOVE
TONIGHT'
FROM *THE LION KING*
ORIGINAL SONG
MUSIC BY ELTON JOHN
LYRICS BY TIM RICE

1994

*A profusion of wayward red and orange tulips spill over in sweet disorder onto the lapis lazuli, malachite and porphyry segments incorporated in a specimen marble table.*

*The rose was the symbol of the god of love, Eros, and is also Elton's favourite flower. Against a dramatic, blood-red background of 'Ecstasy' and 'Nicole' roses, two early nineteenth-century cupids quarrel over the plump heart lying between them. Beneath the fighting couple a set of ten Dresden cherubs are playing in a sea of strewn rose petals.*

*The sun floods onto a round table covered with flowers and objets d'art in Elton's private sitting room in his suite in the country house. An antiqued, verdigris-bronze statue in the form of a dancing faun, after the original discovered at Pompeii, is flanked by an arrangement of brick-coloured 'Leonora' roses, lilies, deep-magenta dahlias, gerberas and branches of spindleberry laden with pink berries. On the left lies Bear Pond, a book of nudes pictured in natural surroundings by the famous American photographer Bruce Weber.*

are the flowers requiring a close inspection before they consent to reveal their innermost secret beauty'. A verse of Elton's bittersweet song, 'Curtains', written in collaboration with his longtime musical partner and lyricist, Bernie Taupin, seems evocative of the pastel dreams of childhood:

*Cultivate the freshest flower*
*This garden ever grew,*
*Beneath these branches*
*I once wrote such childish words for you.*
*But that's okay.*
*There's treasure children always seek to find,*
*And just like us*
*You must have had*
*A Once Upon A Time.*

*In a quiet corner of the drawing room at Woodside hangs a striking painting of an equestrian nobleman, possibly a member of the Thurn and Taxis family, by Johann Georg de Hamilton (1672–1737). The painting, in its superb gilded frame, was purchased by Elton from the estate of the late Jackie Kennedy Onassis, who was herself a superb equestrian. It discreetly complements the rich tones of the fine, polished wood. The rider's scarlet coat is picked up in the colour of the small vase of 'Ecstasy' roses on the splendid, eighteenth-century Dutch walnut bombe commode with its claw-and-ball feet. Flanking the commode on either side are a pair of eighteenth-century Dutch dining chairs, made in walnut and covered in floral marquetry; including a Bacchus mask with a parrot and a flowering urn. One feels that Mrs Onassis would have thoroughly approved of the setting.*

Fairy tales, flowers and folklore are interwoven in many of our childhood memories, and centuries of widespread belief in the power of flowers and plants is embedded in our adult consciousness. Despite the rich nectar of our folklore, we have forgotten many of the origins of plant use. Few remember that holly was originally brought into the house as a protector against evil, or that grey-green mistletoe, with its clusters of tiny pearl-moon berries, must always be treated with great respect lest one is killed, like the unfortunate Balder the Beautiful – his mother had overlooked obtaining an oath of protection from it 'because it seemed too young to swear not to hurt her son'.

Besides ensuring their rightful place in people's affections as plants of virtue – healing our spirits and bodies since the time of the ancients – in the spiralling mists of myth and legend many flowering plants have associations with magic: fairies and elves, witches and devils, toads and snakes. There is a multitude of vernacular names which a single flower can possess – 'faeries' spindles', 'witches thimbles', 'elf-shot' and 'devil's bit' (which, if picked, ensure the arrival of the devil at your bedside at night) and the darkly beautiful, poisonous, snake's head fritillaries with their demurely hanging cups. The foxglove – the symbol of insincerity – is a goblin or fairy's flower, and many tales from Ireland, where belief in the 'little people' is still fervent, have been passed down through the generations. Irish women once held a strong belief that the foxglove was the only flowering plant guaranteed to bring back children who had been stolen by the fairies.

However successful their magical properties, flowers are undeniably some of nature's most artful creations. As well as luring bees and butterflies, birds

*A single, perfect dusty-red 'Leonora' rose opens its petals to the sun.*

*… My garden all is overblown with roses,*
*My spirit all is overblown with rhyme,*
*As like a drunked boneybee I waver*
*From house to garden and again to house,*
*And, undetermined which delight to favour,*
*On verse and rose alternately carouse.*

SONNET –
VITA SACKVILLE-WEST.

*High on a throne of royal state, which far*
*Outshone the wealth of Ormus and of Ind,*
*Or where the gorgeous East with richest hand*
*Showers on her kings barbaric pearl and gold.*

PARADISE LOST –
MILTON.

*There are few places in a house which can be as romantic and as inviting as a tented kelim room. Under the eaves of Elton's country house, a dramatic, damask-rose tent filled with kelim carpets and plump cushions is readied for an evening with friends. Fresh gerbera flowers are entwined through the delicate fretwork of the Moroccan hanging lamp which subtly lights the feast below. A brass-tray table is filled to overflowing with mouth-watering delicacies from the East – brass bowls of Turkish delight and dates, figs and pistachios; sugar lumps in the shape of hearts and diamonds. An elegant, nineteenth-century 'ewer' coffee pot stands between two of the four hand-painted enamel glasses which are filled with perfumed tea – a single rose petal has been placed in each glass.*

and beetles, to help in their procreation, they have fascinated humans so deeply that they have been carried across oceans and deserts on voyages which would have defeated their pollen alone. But there are also flowers on everyone's hit list, including Elton's – floral numbers which could never reach the 'Top of the Pops':

*There are certain flowers which I simply can't abide – chrysanthemums, which remind me of death and which I absolutely refuse to have in my hotel rooms. I loathe baby's breath and I'm not very fond of carnations. I can't stand them in a vase or on their own and I can't believe men actually wear them in their buttonholes. The only place where they are pretty and should remain is in a garden. I also dislike the scent of jonquils and narcisssus.*

Ancient superstitions regarding plants have lingered on for centuries. A medieval legend in Europe has it that when the Virgin Mary lay upon a crude bed of bracken and lady's bedstraw 'Bracken refused to acknowledge the child and lost its flower, Lady's bedstraw welcomed the child and, blossoming at that moment, found that its flowers had changed from white to gold'. During the first half of this century the practice persisted in a valley in Germany of women placing lady's bedstraw in their beds to ease the hazards and pain of childbirth. And

The elegant stairway in the hall at Woodside is dressed up for the Christmas festivities. Graceful swags of deep-crimson velvet intermingle with fir branches, fir cones, cinnamon sticks and bunches of fresh, ruby 'Sasha' roses. A mass of red amaryllis, poinsettia, scarlet ilex berries, 'Only Love' roses and contorted willow twigs peak out from the windowsill, while a French, eighteenth-century tapestry hanging on the wall above completes the welcoming tableau.

Elton looks forward to the excitement of Christmas, and to placing the mass of presents under the tree in the dining room. Each year the tree is dressed according to a different theme. Here it is laden with white Tiffany balls and bells, as well as with sparkling antique ornaments from Milan – fat jewels of gold and silver like a tree in a fairy tale. The fairy on top of the tree is a Kenny angel, without his Barbie, dressed in a blush-white gown and pearls. On his head is placed a golden crown, and his gossamer wings allow him to float above the tree.

*An old red telephone box in the woodland is home to a sylph-like female statue. Perhaps waiting patiently for her lover to call, she amuses herself by swathing her body in luscious pink camellias.*

*Ginger flowers grace a Melbourne tram bought on a whim during an Australian concert tour, and now David's office in the garden. 'That was bought in the cocaine days', Elton says.*

since new mothers were believed to be vulnerable to attack from demons, they refused to enter a house without a few strands of lady's bedstraw in their shoes.

Elton laughed at the suggestion that his mother, Sheila, may have done the same. His affection for this woman – who is warm-hearted and bursting with vitality – is still powerfully evident as he dwells on their close, loving relationship: '

*As I explained in David's documentary on me, I think I have always been a mummy's boy. My mum was the one person, besides my gran and my aunt, whom I could always rely on for support and for love when I was young, so I am incredibly attached to my mother. Absolutely nobody has stood by me or continuously been there for me like she has.*

# Blue & Mauve

… *But the sun rolling high*
*Through the sapphire sky*
*Keeps great and small*
*onthe endless round*
*… It's the circle of life*

'The Circle of Life' – music by Elton John,
lyrics by Tim Rice

*A delicate 1930s glass-*
*mirrored piano nestling*
*in a mass of hydrangeas,*
*reflects the petals in the*
*open bevelled top.*

*As a kid, you're always made to mow the lawn. I didn't mind*

*mowing, but weeding I hated. I've always liked gardens and I've*

*always loved flowers, but I haven't got green fingers at all.*

ELTON JOHN.

*Like a child's random painting, a bright-blue-and-purple flower with green leaves and stem grows steadily out of a flowerpot. The picture is made up of a few of Elton's many pairs of shoes and suits. A posy of pale-lilac scabious and violacea from his garden, mixed with hydrangea and blue lisianthus, form the centre of the fantasy flower which stretches out towards the beaming sun. The exotic petals and green leaves are made up of blue suede shoes, satin lilac boots, iridescent bluey-greens, silk evening slippers and patent purple numbers. Various blue-and-green Versace suits in shiny PVC, sequins, soft silk velvets and green snakeskin print form the fantasy picture's rolling sky and grass.*

This poem, 'Piano', by D H Lawrence, is a favourite of Elton's. Hanging in his kitchen, it is a poignant reminder of his own musical beginnings.

*Softly, in the dusk, a woman is singing to me,*
*Taking me back down the vista of years, till I see*
*A child sitting under the piano, in the boom of the tingling strings*
*And pressing the small, poised feet of a mother*
*Who smiles as she sings.*

*In spite of myself, the insidious mastery of song,*
*Betrays me back, till the heart of me weeps to belong*
*To the old Sunday evenings at home, with winter outside*
*And hymns in the cosy parlour, the tinkling piano our guide.*

*So now it is vain for the singer to burst into clamour*
*With the great black piano appassionate. The glamour*
*Of childish days is upon me, my manhood is cast*
*Down in the flood of remembrance, I weep like a child for the past.*

*A seventeenth-century Flemish limewood cherub sitting nonchalantly with his legs crossed on an oak bracket on the wall, gazes over a quiet scene in the gallery. Besides a large vase of pale-and dark-mauve delphiniums, the dominant feature in the room is a stately, French, nineteenth-century 'Grecian' harp, whose fluted column is decorated at the top with three tapering female terms. One of a pair of nineteenth-century, bronze, winged putti points his right index finger down to the original score for Elton's song 'Soul Glove' while the score for 'Wrap Her Up' lies on the floor.*

Born on 25 March 1947, the childhood and adolescence of Reginald Dwight, as Elton had been christened, was spent in the sublime ordinariness of Pinner, Middlesex, a north London suburb. The place has remained largely unchanged, with the ghost of a Victorian gentility slipping away like a fading patient. Elton recalls:

*I didn't have an unhappy childhood. Overall, it was pretty good. As a kid I was really interested in collecting records and all of them were in pristine condition. I was quite shy, so I used to retreat to my room and create my own fantasy world. I remember collectables were quite important to me, but in those days that meant little Dinky and Matchbox toys, all of which were kept in perfect order. I would never, ever, let anyone borrow any of my records. I wrote my name on the cover of the record and also wrote the number down and filed it. I have got that kind of mind —anally retentive beyond belief. And I knew the publisher of the records. I have always found that interesting and have carried the habit on into my later life.*

*The vivid colours of lavender sweet peas and scabious blue, together with rich purple lisianthus, spring out in sweet disorder from a Lalique vase. A favourite antique gilt-and-glass box of Elton's, along with a silver-framed photo of himself and his partner David, stand out against the striking marquetry design of the satin-birch table.*

Robert Louis Stevenson's poem seems tailor-made for the young boy:

*When I am grown to Man's Estate*
*I shall be very proud and great.*
*And tell the other girls and boys*
*Not to meddle with my toys.*

Elton, shy and polite, grew up under the devoted eye of Sheila Dwight, his mother, and his grandmother, Ivy Sewell, both of whom constantly encouraged and consoled him. Although Sheila has remained the 'abiding influence on me', Elton recognizes that 'the pivotal person in my life was my grandmother'.

*Even though there wasn't much money around, she made the most of everything and was constantly there in my life. She was a great character, loved travelling and was staying with me on her first trip to Los Angeles when I tried to commit suicide by taking sleeping pills and throwing myself into the swimming pool. She played cards and was as sharp as a button, although sometimes she pretended she wasn't. I love old people. Old people and kids tell you the truth and they don't care because they don't have any hidden agendas. At least they say what they think. I used to feel uncomfortable with that, but now I don't. The older I get the less rubbish I tolerate … don't be cloying, don't say anything unnecessary and don't lie.*

Elton's elegant, mint-green silk shoes have an air of the Elizabethan dandy about them. But instead of lace and satin, they are topped by an extravagant ruffle of cerise cyclamens.

Although he admits, when asked if he always says what is on his mind: 'No, not really. I've always kept it inside. But now I'm getting better at getting it out. Yes, Yes. YES!'

For years Elton harboured a certain bitterness towards his remote, absentee father, a squadron leader in the Royal Air Force:

My early life was based on fear. And fear is the worst thing you can instil in someone. I suppose it comes from my father, whom I was frightened of, always fearful, which made me drop things. I always wanted to do things to please him – trying not to make a mistake because I knew the next day I would get rapped for it. I think if you are a boy you want a special relationship with your dad. I wish I had had that ability to bond with my father, but I didn't. And for a while I blamed him for it.

'I was too young to understand the chemistry between my father and my mother. But they did the best they could. I had everything given to me. For the last three or four years of their marriage they stayed together for my education when they were obviously very unhappy, which was an unselfish thing to do. But actually I think I would have preferred it if they had split up.

'A bowl of blue hydrangeas resting on a Biedermeier table in front of shelves filled with Elton's Ivor Novello music awards add a colourful touch. Photos of Elton are scattered around his custom-built beech, rosewood and ebonised library. The black satin-and-moire striped sofa, with its antique needlepoint cushions, adds a cosy touch to a dramatic room.

The piano-wire tension between his parents eventually led to a divorce when Elton was fifteen, with his mother later marrying a man who proved a model stepfather. But being brought up in an almost exclusively feminine milieu was bound to have had an impact:

*I think that fact shaped me a lot when I was growing up. It made me feel a bit of a loner. I simply didn't want anyone to enter my world. But now, knowing my father is dead, I don't hold a grudge. He tried the best he could. And he had four more kids after he remarried and was a very good father to them.*

Sentiments of absence and solitude spin through the silver threads of Elton's song 'Emily':

*…In a cage sits a gold canary
By a wicker chair and a rosewood loom
As a soul ascends aboard the evening
Canary sings to an empty room …*

*Fresh from Elton's garden, burgundy-, deep-purple and wine-coloured sweet peas fill a brass-and-copper, Regency fire grate, which has been cleverly turned into a stylish basin in the Orangery's cloakroom. An old copper-beater living nearby took over one hundred hours to beat the metal into shape before it was enamelled. The captivating result stands on a granite plinth, and is set off by two antique, French, lapis-lazuli-and-gilt bas-reliefs.*

It takes a rare soul to sense that flowers, like children, may also flourish in the company and approval of others. Many years ago, when former King Ferdinand of Bulgaria created a ravishing garden of Japanese plants at his palace on the Black Sea, he feared that the flowers might feel lonely, so Japanese butterflies were imported to keep them from pining. This companionable spirit can occasionally overstep the mark, as it did in the case of the English writer, Walter Savage Landor, a man of furious temper. Throwing his cook out of the window and into a flower bed, he was heard to

*Turn me loose from your hands*

bellow: 'Good God! I forgot the violets.'

It was in those solitary hours of growing up that Elton found what was to

*Let me fly to distant lands*

be his most constant companion, the family piano. Even as a toddler, who often played a piece after a single hearing, his perfect musical ear suggested astonishing precocity. In 1995 he stated in his moving acceptance speech on winning an Oscar for his song 'Can You Feel The Love Tonight', for the Walt Disney cartoon feature film *The Lion King*:'I would like to dedicate this to

*Over green fields, trees and mountains*

my grandmother, Ivy Sewell, who died last week. She was the one who sat me down at the piano when I was three and made me play. So I am accepting this in her honour.' Elton recalls his moment of glory: 'Although most award

*Flowers and forest fountains*

shows are pretty boring because the award itself is boring, the Oscars is something special. Receiving the golden statue was one of the proudest moments of my life. I loved doing the film because it was for kids. An added bonus was that my parents were there and I was able to say goodbye to my

*Home along the lanes of the skyway.*

nan.' Soon after their joint triumph, Tim Rice, his collaborator and lyricist, expressed his admiration for Elton: 'He's one of the great composers of the whole century, I think.'

At Pinner County Grammar School (he still keeps his old brown blazer's badge, with its rearing stag above the motto 'Honour before Honours' as a glass paperweight on the desk in his study), Elton was an imaginative, if earnest, pupil, who preferred to save his considerable energies for the Steinway piano in the assembly hall. He recalls: 'In those days I used to practice the piano for hours, always lugging round my satchel, which was stuffed with musical scores by Brahms, Mozart and Chopin, my favourite composer.' Harbouring a penchant for neatness, he began a childhood

'SKYLINE PIGEON'
— MUSIC BY
ELTON JOHN,
LYRICS BY TAUPIN.

*This small garden was designed by Rosemary Verey. The seemingly random placement of flowers and plants brings the area into harmony with its natural surroundings.*

A magnificent, cut-glass
chandelier in the
Georgian style, touched
by soft sprays of lilac
delphinium, 'Delila' roses
and copper-coloured
prunus, greets visitors in
the high-ceilinged hall of
Elton's country house.
The chandelier, with its
numerous, swan-necked
curves, festoons and
pendulum drops, frames
the dark-eyed face of a
lady in the equally
elegant Lavery painting
on the wall, The Black
Poodle (1905). Elton is a
great lover and collector
of portraits, including
several by Gainsborough,
and this large, dramatic
painting remains a
favourite of his.

pattern which was carried over into adult life. 'I write a diary, but it's really boring. I never write anything personal in it for fear it might get stolen. But I am a great list-maker and am always listing things down. I *adore* making lists and constantly jot down my record sales in a special book with all the figures colour-coded.' His solitary adolescence led him later to admit: 'I grew up with inanimate objects as my friends and I still believe they have feelings. That's why I keep hold of my possessions. I'll look at them and remember when they gave me a bit of happiness.' This sense of isolation and insecurity has now lessened since his latest fresh start. 'My self esteem is so much better now. I'm definitely cracking it, but forty-three years of insecurity isn't going to change overnight.'

The year 1962 brought with it an avalanche of Beatlemania, sweeping Britain off its feet. Gripped by rock 'n' roll, and inspired by the lads from Liverpool, Elton, the unassuming classical music buff who had already won a prestigious scholarship to the Royal Academy of Music in London, was by

A single, pale-lilac
scabious flower appears
out of the dark gloaming
of antique Roman glass
bottles in Elton's
bedroom. The fragile
collection includes the
slender, amethyst-tinted
flask with delicate, blue-
glass handles in the
foreground. Mainly
translucent, the
mulberry-wine,
iridescent-blue and sea-
grey-coloured bottles
stand on a tall chest
designed by David Linley.

*The fireplace in the drawing room at Woodside is suffused with golden light from the hall and the dining room on either side. A painting of Windsor Castle by Patrick Naysmith (1826) hanging above the fire surround reminds one how near Elton lives to one of the queen's favourite castles. A magnificent, nineteenth-century Meissen clock has pride of place on the mantlepiece. The porcelain case is covered with delicate shells, scrolls and sprays*

*of summer flowers, including Elton's beloved roses. A mass of mostly mid-nineteenth-century Staffordshire leopards on green, grassy bases – Elton's favourite collectables, which he loves to find personally – either stride or laze across the mantlepiece. A profusion of purple- and lilac-coloured gladioli, delphinium and scabious, combined with lisianthus, rosy-red-and mauve-coloured violacea add their vibrant colours to the ordered room.*

now pounding away at the keys and letting rip with true Jerry Lee Lewis gusto – much to his schoolmates' amazement. As he gained confidence, so his abilities as a born showman, gifted mimic and comedian developed. Wider horizons beckoned. Any thoughts of becoming a concert pianist flew rapidly out of the classroom window, and on leaving school, Elton took a job playing the piano on Saturday nights in a local pub:

*It's such an advantage when you know what you want to do at an early age. I knew that all I really wanted to do was get into the music business. I didn't care how, or what I did. But a lot of my friends went to university and got their degrees. Then they came out and they didn't know what they wanted to do and just ambled through their lives.*

This dedication fuelled the tenuous start to Elton's eventual rise to fame and fortune. In those dizzy days of the 1960s, the wild men of rock who, besides the Beatles, would personify that era - the Rolling Stones, Rod Stewart, Eric Clapton and The Who – were about to storm the world. In 1967 Reggie Dwight changed his less than glamorous name, purloining his new name from the tenor-sax player in his Bluesology band, Elton Dean, and the high camp blues singer, Long John Baldry. Looking back, Elton muses:

*I can't say that flowers have influenced my music in any way other than having them around when I am figuring out a melody. Perhaps they have influenced Bernie because he is a very country person. Lincolnshire, where he comes from, is 'spud' land really – very flat and not the most beautiful part of England – so, being a sensitive soul, flowers probably mattered to him.*

Flowers and music have continuously danced through the lyrics of poets through the centuries. Shakespeare, in this verse from Henry VIII, penned:

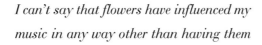

*Orpheus with his lute made trees,*
*    And the mountain-tops that freeze*
*Bow themselves when he did sing:*
*    To his music plants and flowers*
*Ever sprung; as sun and showers*
*    There had made a lasting spring.*

*The sweet-smelling perfume of wild violets has delighted us for more than 2,000 years. As the violet's heady scent suggested the art of love-making, so it became the flower of the goddess Aphrodite. Here, on a butler's table in the drawing room, deep-purple violets are delicately entwined like a purple daisy chain around a favourite collection of heart-shaped Limoges boxes.*

*He must have been a gardener*

*that cared a lot*

*Who weeded out the tears*

*and grew a good crop*

'EMPTY GARDEN
(HEY HEY JOHNNY)'
– MUSIC BY ELTON JOHN,
LYRICS BY TAUPIN.

Although Elton's music is likely to stir different sensibilities to Orpheus's, perhaps his too inspires the flowering plants around him. Music and flowers share a common bond – both enrich our lives by making us happier. Together they celebrate special and joyful occasions – festivals, ceremonies and rites of passage. Dances are often transformed into unforgettable events with sumptuous bowers of roses and scented garlands cascading from balconies. Our custom of dancing round a garlanded maypole, crowning a maiden queen of the May with a wreath of blossoms and seating her upon a throne of flowers, stems back to Beltane, the ancient pagan festival of sacrifice and purification. Renamed May Day, the rite paid homage to spring, with people going out into the countryside with songs and music to bring back 'the May' into villages and towns. Apart from being the May tree, as well as a lover's tree in poetry, the hawthorn – one of the most magical of all flowering trees – has always been a symbol of sex and fertility. Its numerous magical properties are made infinitely more potent by the night dew – itself a magic liquid – on the eve before May day, providing protection against the spiteful ways of fairies and witches, creatures who are constantly active on the actual day.

Elton's favourite flower, the rose, has long been associated with music

*Elton's* jardin potager, *or picking garden, in the country is filled with flowers, vegetables and fruit. In late summer, numerous plum trees are laden down with sweet, round fruit, ready for plucking. The early morning sun filters through a cluster of purple plums, catching in its rays the delicate, filigree web of a spider.*

*The large, silver-blue leaves of the salvia 'Argentinia' plant catch the morning dew on their soft, downy surfaces as they lie like plump velvet cushions in the early autumn sun.*

and dance. In the Middle Ages, troubadours, who wandered the land as lyric composers and poets, recognized the rose as the symbol of both universal love and Christianity. This delicate beauty also gave its name to the ballet *Le Spectre de la Rose*, in which Nijinsky first danced the spirit of the rose, dressed in an elaborate costume of rose petals. Although as a friend of royalty, celebrities, the cellist Rostropovich, and the glitterati, dancing may not head the list of Elton's favourite occupations, but he occasionally indulges in a quick whirl across the dance floor. He recalled afterwards in an interview of a dance with Princess Anne at Prince Andrew's twenty-first birthday party at Windsor Castle: 'As we're bobbing up and down, the Queen comes up with an equerry and says: "Do you mind if we join you?" Just at that moment the music segues into Bill Haley's "Rock Around the Clock". So there I am dancing to "Rock around the Clock" with the Queen of England.'

Unlike Elton, who happens to be highly articulate as well as one of the most successful singing stars of all times, not every rock musician boasts such a keen sense of humour. Elton is reknowned for being witty, quick and often wildly funny, with a better

*The female statue at the entrance to the swimming pool in the country looks as if she has just put on her stole of flowers to keep the cold night air from harming her. A medley of dusty-pink 'Black Tea' roses, powdery-lilac 'Bluebird' roses and small 'Souplesse' roses combine with 'La Rêve' lilies, mauve and white ornamental cabbages and purple Michaelmas daisies. All the flowers are entwined with vine leaves and ivy. The result is a stunningly effective way in which to dress up a statue.*

*A bunch of cerise-coloured sweet peas rests between a collection of antique Lalique vases.*

*A profusion of deep-mauve anemones, dark-blue lisianthus and lilac and blue hyacinths spring up from the background of Elton's luscious, gold-and-purple, silk Versace dressing gown. Nestling in the folds are two Prussian-blue and gold Murano glass vases, a plate and a goblet.*

deadpan delivery than Truman Capote. At times his humour is laced with self-mockery, at others it is playfully high camp; when 'he' often lapses into 'she'; when Mick Jagger becomes Mrs Jagger. The last to entrance audiences, friends and interviewers in much the same vein was John Lennon. My own introduction to Elton's swift repartee occurred one day at Woodside when he about to start a brisk game of tennis with his coach. Dressed in crisp white shorts and carrying a tennis racket and balls, Elton cheerily greeted those of us standing in the courtyard, bent down to pat one of his nine dogs and promptly dropped one of the tennis balls. 'Not the first time I've dropped me balls,' he cracked, without missing a beat.

'As far as humour is concerned, I find people around me like Bob Halley, my personal assistant who has been with me for the past twenty-two years, very funny,' Elton remarks, also noting that 'without Bob, I would be dead by now'.

A sea of woodland bluebells is caressed by dappled sunlight.

A purple, braided, velvet footstool is festooned with gold and purple beads threaded onto gold and black tasselling, and is finished off with intricate ribbons and grey-green silk rope.

We are always laughing amongst ourselves and we're very self-deprecating, which is good. Actually I think living in England is altogether pretty self-deprecating, because people won't let you get too big for your boots. I love crazy, brilliantly written humour like 'Fawlty Towers', 'The Good Life' or 'Black Adder'. Although I hate stand-up comedians, I find people like Billy Connolly funny. English humour is definitely the best. I don't find too many people in America particularly funny except Whoopi Goldberg and Robin Williams, who I think is a genius. The trouble is, few Americans have any sense of irony. If half of those American film stars, who are perceived as royalty, lived over here they would be torn to bits. People simply wouldn't tolerate their notorious behaviour.

# Yellow & Peach

*So goodbye yellow-brick road,*

*Where the dogs of society howl,*

*You can't plant me in your penthouse,*

*I'm going back to my plough.*

'GOODBYE YELLOW-BRICK ROAD' –
MUSIC BY ELTON JOHN, LYRICS BY TAUPIN.

*A pair of Elton's red Versace shoes are about to dance up the yellow brick road made out of yellow chrysanthemums, surrounded by fields of moss, rose leaves, ivy, and the bobbing heads of green chrysanthemums. A bright-red euphorbia sun blazes out of a blue chrysanthemum sky. The large tree in the foreground is fashioned out of euphorbia leaves, and cypress trees of rhododendron leaves are placed randomly in the fields.*

*Woodside is the hub of my soul*
*probably. It is the centre of my life. My*
*other houses – Queensdale in London,*
*Atlanta and the South of France are*
*like appendages to the tree.*

ELTON JOHN.

For Elton, Woodside expresses his most fundamental idea of home:

*I love coming home, back to England, to this house. It give me a sense of peace. When I*
*go on tour people often say to me 'How can you bear to leave Woodside?' I tell them that*
*the only way I can is knowing I can come back to it. I go through those gates, knowing*
*I'm going away for three or four months and think 'God, how much I long to get back'.*
*When I do, I see the garden changing – there's always something magical happening*
*here.*

Bought in 1975, Woodside is a three-storey, labyrinthine Queen Anne-style house situated on the outskirts of the village of Old Windsor, surrounded by thirty-seven acres of rolling Berkshire countryside in which deer, dogs and a donkey, plus the odd pheasant, roam. Although it has burnt down three times since it was first built (the last time soon after World War II), parts of it date back to the sixteenth century, when it was King Henry VIII's physician's dwelling. Since Windsor Castle can be clearly seen from the top of the house, the king would order the flag to be hoisted or bonfires and flares lit whenever his gout was giving him trouble, enabling the good doctor to leap onto his horse and attend his patient. 'The queen mother says I've easily got the best view of Windsor Castle in the whole of Berkshire', Elton remarks. His penchant for the pleasures of domesticity permeates the lyrics of his song 'Your Song':

*An enchantingly pretty medley of yellow garden and pinky-peach 'Queen Beatrix' roses, combined with sprigs of mauve catmint, shelters a few pieces from Elton's vast collection of china pug dogs in his private sitting room. The decoration of morning-glory and sweet peas on the vase accentuates the lightness of the flowers in comparison with the Limoges, Meissen, Dresden and Staffordshire animals covering the carved-scroll capital of the solid, Biedermeier-style, cherrywood, pedestal cupboard. The walls of the sitting room are covered with a superb collection of paintings by Henry Scott Tuke (1858–1929). Elton owns one of the most important collections of Tuke's paintings in the world. To the left of the table can be seen* The Back of Charlie *and* Two Boys on a Beach.

It's a little bit funny, this feeling inside

I'm not one of those that can easily hide

I don't have much money, but boy if I did

I'd buy a big house where we both could live.

*I am basically a home-loving person and I feel now that this house is full of love. But as I have said before, it used to be a rampant party house with a great deal of drugs being taken. Although it had beautiful things in amongst the most awful crap, it was a pretty unhappy house. It was a total mishmash – full of furniture, leather Chesterfields, Tiffany lamps and jukeboxes, pinball machines, stuffed animals and dumb things like lamps and vases stacked on the floor because I had nowhere to put them. You couldn't sit down. Once I became sober I realized that I simply didn't want that anymore, so I changed it completely – it was knocked down and redesigned. I wanted a house that was comfortable, where people could come and stay; that was full of love and peace. I think that is what this house is about.*

*In a secluded niche next to the chapel, an eighteenth-century, marble statue of Pan, bought at Sotheby's (one of a pair in the Orangery), plays a melody on his pipes. Creamy, yellow roses and 'Evergreen' honeysuckle are entwined around both him and the goat which lies protectively at his feet.*

David Furnish concurs: 'Elton is very proud of his houses. After coming out of rehabilitation he wanted to get rid of the rock-star image – he had been very unhappy in those days. So he shed all the rock-star glitter. He's now very happy and so am I. Far happier than we were before we met.'

'China tea, the scent of hyacinths, wood fires, and bowls of violets – that is my mental picture of an agreeable February afternoon' wrote the late Constance Spry, the ultimate English flower-arranger. This description could easily apply to a cosy afternoon at Woodside, in which every room is in pristine order; where the former discothèque, with its mirrored ball and attendant amyl nitrite, is now a serene drawing room, resplendent with chintzy sofas, muted colours and antiques, and the glitzy private cinema has been transformed into a comfortable sitting room for viewing the latest videos. On first stepping into

Woodside's large entrance hall – which is devoid of unnecessary paraphernalia and mirrors the bare, empty rooms of the eighteenth century – one has entered a house exuding both personal warmth and tranquility. Looking around the drawing room, the words of the interior designer Mario Praz come to mind: 'By a subtle and inevitable process, the man who cares for his house can easily become a collector.' On Regency card tables, rich sapphire lisianthus mixed with the butterfly-like petals of yellow garden roses, lilies, and cerise gerberas, spring like crescent rainbows out of cut-glass vases. Large, terracotta pots filled with forests of muddy-pink cymbidium orchids grace a corner of the room. (Because of its pair of ball-shaped root-tubers, *Orchis* means testicle. The prudish John Ruskin was so horrified at discovering this that he suggested that the plant be rechristened 'wreathewort'.) Always meticulously tidy, Elton's discriminating eye knows the fixed position of every single photo, family memento, book and *objet d'art*. Years ago he commented on his craving for order: 'I hoover and dust. I used to love ironing too. It soothed me. Always emptying ashtrays, washing and putting them away.'

Having spent numerous years buying on an epic scale, every room now appears comfortably full without being overcrowded. A great variety of antiques, paintings and objects, unrelated but sympathetic, give each room its individual personality and style. The eye is pleased and the senses caressed:

*As the sunflowers turns to her god when he sets The same look which she turned when he rose.*

THOMAS MOORE.

*At one end of the small cloakroom sits a stupendously theatrical, deep-crimson velvet throne. The feel of the design is purely medieval. A burst of sunflowers in a pewter vase below the bronze pull captures the light flooding in from the oval window.*

*The rich tones of Jean Ranc's (1674–1735) painting of a nobleman, and the Regency gilt mirror bring a formal elegance to the sunny, melon-coloured walls of the London drawing room. On the mantlepiece a Louis XVI clock is flanked by two Regency candelabra. Two French, stone poodles stand either side of the fireplace, as if to protect the flowers within. A profusion of gold euphorbia, cream lisianthus, butter-yellow amaryllis and roses is framed by the white marble, almost resembling a painting on its own. Beneath the mirror, drawings and photos in intricate velvet and gilt frames sit neatly on top of a Biedermeier Empire console decorated with two bronze, female, Egyptian figures with gilded wings.*

*Roy Strong, the former director of the Victoria and Albert Museum, once told me that although everyone is so obsessed with buying old things, it is equally important to own beautiful new things as well, so that one day they can become the antiques of this age. I think he has a very valid point. John Biles, an extraordinarily talented furniture-maker has made many of the things in my houses, including the dining-room table and the sideboard, the library at Queensdale and numerous things in the Orangery.*

Being a man who is particularly visually aware, and one who pays great attention to detail, it is no surprise that architecture is one of Elton's passions:

*British architects often don't revere our cultural heritage, unlike in France and Italy, where people feel far more passionately about preserving their own culture. The Italians really were in tears when the opera house in Venice burnt down –*

it was an absolute tragedy for them. I know Paris wasn't bombed in the war, but we would give the thumbs down to what they have done with the Louvre and the Musée D'Orsay. Carbuncles are continually being built next to beautiful old buildings – our new British Library is a disgrace. I can't think of one modern building in London which I like.

However, the stress of rebuilding his own house is indelibly stamped on his memory:

*Andrew Protheroe and Adrian Cooper-Grigg did a wonderful job of redesigning, although after a year and a half I thought I must be stark, staring mad. I came down here when it was almost finished, and it was just a sea of mud – you've never seen anything like it. But it's amazing how quickly things come together once all the building work is done. I don't suppose things are ever completely finished. If you're interested in design, fabrics, flowers and decoration in houses, there's always something to do because there are always things you want to change. That aspect fascinates me, because as you get older I think your eye gets better. Your taste changes. When I first started collecting I adored Art Nouveau, so I collected it by the lorry load. Now I am keen on other things.*

*A group of Meissen allegorical amorini, all infant boys in the pursuit of love, greet Elton as he steps into his private apartment in the country. They stand on a Regency, satinwood- and rosewood-veneered side table. Each of the charming figurines wears a differently coloured drape, and most are busy with a small, plump, peach-coloured heart – caressing, watering, hammering, piercing, decorating. A small posy of soft-yellow garden roses nestles amongst the amorini, across the front of each of which words of love are written in pink script . . . 'Je les rends legers', 'Je le dompte', 'Je blesse et soulage', 'Je les unis'. In the background stand six equally delicately coloured cupids.*

Elton was forty-one when he decided to jettison twenty-years' worth of collectables and revert to a traditional look for Woodside.

*I had so much stuff and sold practically everything in 1989, except about five paintings – a Magritte, a Francis Bacon and a couple by Patrick Proctor. I gave away my Rembrandt etching,* The Adoration of the Shepherds, *to Rod Stewart. I don't see him very often as he lives in Los Angeles, but he's an old friend. I was very lucky, selling at just the right time before things went a little sour. And for someone who had always grown up loving things, it was an incredibly cleansing experience.*

The surface of Elton's mahogany partner's desk in his study is crammed full of photographs of himself with friends, including Elizabeth Taylor; Diana, Princess of Wales; Ronald Reagan; the pop group, Take That; plus an amusing one taken with the stars of the television series 'Absolutely Fabulous', Joanna Lumley and Jennifer Saunders, in which Elton, not to be outdone in the glamour department, is wearing a platinum wig. The Oscar which Elton won for the song 'Can you feel the love tonight' from The Lion King *(see page 20)* takes pride of place on the brown-leather desktop. A further prized possession is the stunning jade, gold and lapis-lazuli clock in the shape of an elephant. It is studded with precious and semi-precious stones, and was given to Elton by Prince Abdul Hakeem of Brunei. It gives the time in New York, Brunei and London. A miniature, old-fashioned, brass phonograph sits near the front, with the inscription :

NATIONAL ACADEMY OF
RECORDING ARTS AND
SCIENCES

DIONNE & FRIENDS
FEATURING
ELTON JOHN,
GLADYS KNIGHT &
STEVIE WONDER

BEST POP PERFORMANCE
BY A DUO OR GROUP
WITH VOCAL – 1986

*'That's what
friends are for'.*

Water ripples invitingly in Elton's key-patterned Jacuzzi in the swimming-pool area in the country. The dancing rays of a watery sun, made from yellow-, apricot-, and gold-coloured gerbera lined with glowing night-candles are laid out on the cool, stone floor as if to say 'Come on in, it's summer the whole year round'.

*Purple rain has turned to gold*

The celebrity sale at Sotheby's had all the razzmatazz of a rock concert, lasted four days and grossed £14.8 million. Elton readily shares his knowledge of *the clouds of yesterday* fine things with his partner, David Furnish, who says admiringly: 'I have learned a great deal about antiques and paintings since I have been with *And the dandelion dies in the wind.* Elton.' Over the years Elton has cultivated and elevated his taste in his possessions, presently aspiring to country-squire elegance and comfort: 'I've always known what I want in the past, whether it be bad or good. There are always new things at Woodside, like Jackie Kennedy's eighteenth-century equestrian portrait of a nobleman. So I am constantly moving things around.'

Entertaining at home is one of the simple pleasures which Elton enjoys about living in the country. On summer evenings, when his dinner parties are in full swing, the French doors to the stone-paved terrace outside the drawing room are thrown open to catch the cool breeze; the scent of full-blown roses and jasmine rest lightly on the evening air as he and his friends talk into the night: Elton confesses:

'A DANDELION DIES IN THE WIND'
– MUSIC BY ELTON,
LYRICS BY TAUPIN.

*A labyrinthine corridor displays only a few of Elton's platinum and gold discs. In a corner of the corridor at Woodside,* *fresh flowers have been sprayed gold and silver to add a dramatic touch to the surreal spectacle.*

*I hate going to parties. I don't drink any more, so it is very awkward for me to sit and listen to people having a great time. I don't like crowds of people and, the older I get, the less I like it. I've done it for so long it's become a ritual – when I have to 'schmooze', as I call it, although people are usually very pleasant and sometimes don't turn out to be as bad as I think they are going to be. Instead, I like having about forty people down here, maximum. But my favourite situation is to have twelve people to lunch  or dinner, then you can actually talk and exchange ideas. I prefer a mixture of friends and people you haven't met before – that is always the most civilized way to meet someone. There's only one rule I insist on – I never play the piano.*

*It's days like this that you can't resist*
*A long tall drink*
*And a big yellow sun in the winter*

'DANCING IN THE END ZONE' –
MUSIC BY ELTON JOHN,
LYRICS BY TAUPIN.

*This gold-and-russet miniature Limoges piano is one of several owned by Elton.*

*The russet tones of autumn mingle amongst the marigolds and the chocolate plant in a bedroom in the country. An old set of leather cases, including a hatbox and an instrument case which once belonged to a certain Mr Reginald Bastard make a perfect setting for Elton's extravagantly beautiful muff made out of pheasant feathers – a minute bird's head can be seen at the base of the feathers. A charming, French, nineteenth-century lead vase holds sienna-yellow flowers, in front of which rest a pair of highly polished treen boxes in the shape of an apple and a pear.*

The original black Steinway takes pride of place in the drawing room. Now painted such a realistic *faux* walnut that the subterfuge is barely detectable, it is the first piano that Elton ever bought: 'To get a new one done in walnut would have cost an absolute fortune, so I had it painted instead.'

'It's so important to have fresh flowers in a house,' Elton enthuses. His love of them extends from the prized flowers bunched in and out of season by Susie and Julia into every corner of his country home, where the flower motif is in full bloom. This favourite subject has been used decoratively in the applied arts since the beginning of civilization. A tapestry of flowers is strewn on curtains and sofas, embroidered pillows and wallpapers, beadworked Victorian muffs and botanical paintings. Cushions are garlanded with petit-point roses and Tabriz carpets are encrusted with elegant blossoms. Delicate flowers are entwined round his Sèvres and Meissen china, giving a three-

*Now folds the lily all*

*her sweetness up*

*and slips into the*

*bosom of the lake;*

*so fold thyself, my*

*dearest, thou and slip*

*into my bosom, and be*

*lost in me.*

ALFRED, LORD
TENNYSON.

dimensional charm to the individually beautiful pieces, and adorn his numerous small objects, from porcelain, one of his current obsessions, to his favourite possessions – his Staffordshire animals and figurines, 'which I collect personally. I have great fun finding them', says Elton.

Being a collector of quite legendary energy, Elton has, over the years, acquired numerous styles from various periods of paintings – his dining-room walls boast two Gainsboroughs, as well as works by Arthur Devis, the eighteenth century portraitist.

*Elton's London swimming pool, which can be opened up to the sky in warm weather, plunges one back into the spare, linear décor of the l930s. The feel is reminiscent of Cecil Beaton: highly stylized, clean and uncluttered. The arresting mural which fills the wall at the far end was inspired by William Roberts' paintings of statuesque and uninhibited male bathers, relaxing, talking and diving. In this escapist fantasy, sparse branches reaching up for the ceiling are placed in a pair of vast, white urns. Each branch is dotted with salmon-coloured 'Apple Blossom' amaryllis, the symbol of timidity. Joining them on green, velvet thrones in the water are full-blown peonies and waterlilies – the latter the flower of secrecy. It was a cousin of the waterlily; the lotus, which was worshipped by ancient Eyptians, while to Buddhists the lotus symbolizes the purity of humanity's spiritual life.*

*I used to have lots of portraits of me round here, but sold them off. I can't stand going into houses and seeing a portrait of the owner. I think it's tacky. The only person I'd let do a portrait of me would be someone like Julian Schnabel, who does those extraordinary porcelain portraits. I very rarely buy paintings at a gallery because your know you are paying more money than you should. Sometimes you are forced to when you are totally passionate about a painting that you just have to have, but mostly I buy at auctions.*

A favourite artist of Elton's is Henry Scott Tuke (1859–1929), whose work he started collecting six years ago. One of the largest private collections in the world, the paintings hang in Elton's own apartments at Woodside. Tuke's evocative beach scenes and naked youths caught in the natural grace of boyhood are painted with great sensitivity,

*In the London house, a pair of stylish, Art Deco, satinwood and ebony chairs, covered in imitation leopard skin, complement the dramatic painting of a black panther by Paul Jouve, who was active in the late 1800s, which prowls behind them. A small bunch of golden protea, brindled 'Maggie Wee' orchids and cream lisianthus arranged in an exquisite glass vase stands on a chrome table of the modernistic style.*

*The soft yellows of this inviting bedroom and sitting room are set off by the stronger colouring in the floral bed swags, crisp-white damask bedspread and embroidered cushions. A charming, antique, shell vase holds a mass of pure-white Christmas roses, flowers that Spenser refers to in* The Faerie Queene. *An eighteenth-century, English-school portrait,* Lady of the Senhouse Family *, hangs on the wall to the left of the bed.*

*A charming, nineteenth-century lady looks wistfully at her bunch of butter-yellow ranunculus, mimosa and gooseberry-like orange sandersonias. Perhaps they were given to her by a passing admirer.*

constantly reminding one of a gentle, more innocent era. 'I feel a great affinity with him. His paintings are so romantic, yet look so modern. The colours he uses are beautiful. Plus, he was ostracized for what he painted – young boys in boats,' explains Elton. Tuke was part of a group of artists who formed the Newlyn School in Cornwall. It was led by his friend Stanhope Forbes, but because of his subject matter Tuke remained a controversial painter for most of his life; as naked models were rather thin on the ground in Cornwall, he was obliged to hire his principal male model, Johnny, along with a few others, from London.

The delicacy and transient beauty of flowers have inspired numerous artists through the ages. From ancient Chinese scroll paintings and stylistic Egyptian bas-reliefs, to the carved Indian friezes of the Taj Mahal, as well as Persian miniatures, most civilizations have not only enjoyed flowers, but have shown a similar fondness for painting them. Being great flower lovers, it is no surprise that the Chinese were the first people to produce a continuous tradition of flower painting, which was done mainly on silk. The delicacy of the herbs and flowers which were grown for their medicinal properties in the scented medieval kitchen gardens of monasteries, would not only inspire decorative designs and borders for illuminated manuscripts, but would be painted as attributes in religious depictions, especially of the Virgin Mary. However, it was not until the seventeenth century that flowers flooded into paintings, in the art of the Netherlands. The bold expression of colour glowing against a sombre background that was used in Dutch flower painting centred round the tulip, a flower bulb bought in from the Levant during the previous century along with the anemone, the hyacinth and the crocus. Tulips became incredibly popular and 'tulip-mania' caused such slavish devotion that a rare bulb could cost as much as an Amsterdam townhouse.

Some artistic geniuses are partially linked in our minds to the flowers that they painted. Fantin-Latour's sumptuous roses; Odilon Redon's imaginative and poetic floral groupings; van Gogh's sunflowers and irises. Boucher, Fragonard, Watteau and Chardin too all succumbed to the allure of the flower. The Impressionists' use of bright flowers to explore their *'plein air'* aesthetic led Claude Monet to remark: 'I perhaps owe having become a painter to flowers', a remark which could equally apply to Jean-Pierre Redouté, whose watercolours forever preserved the roses in Empress Josephine's garden. The mysterious truths that are embraced within the petals of a small flower inspired the artist Georgia O'Keeffe's sensual paintings: 'Everyone has many associations with a flower – the idea of flowers. You put out your hand to touch the flower – lean forward to smell it – maybe touch it with your lips almost without thinking – or give it to someone to please them.'

One of Elton's favourite places at Woodside is the Orangery which, along with the main house, has been gutted and refurbished. The eighteenth-century building was originally the home of his beloved grandmother, Ivy.

*Just out of sight, two portraits by Gainsborough gaze down at the dining-room table made by John Biles at Woodside, which is laid for one of Elton's sumptuous dinners. Gold-and-white Versace plates, complete with gold napkin rings, are flanked by solid-silver Cartier flatware. Tall vases wrapped in ivy and muslin hold a wonderful profusion of apricot-coloured roses, blush-pink 'Renata' roses,*

*artichokes, 'La Rève' lilies, orange sandasonias, ivy, asparagus and cream lisianthus. The solid-silver male-figured candlesticks and centrepiece holding a luscious medley of fruit and flowers was especially commissioned by Elton and was made by Theo Fennell.*

*The pair of late eighteenth-century, Italian, gilded chairs pictured on the front of Elton's album* Duet *stands in front of the darkly dramatic* Portrait of a Woman *(1987) by the Russian painter Igor Kopystiansky. Elton's gold-studded jacket hangs nonchalantly on the back of one of the chairs.*

*Every time I go into the chapel in the Orangery I feel her presence. She made me very proud. I wanted to build the Orangery as a monument because she was a pivotal figure in my life. My mother always worked, so I spent a lot of the time during the day with my nan. Wherever I went touring in the world, I sent her flowers each week. Living here for fifteen years was idyllic for her, pottering round her own garden in front of the Orangery, which she loved. She was an incredible gardener, and did her own gardening up until the time of her death, growing her roses and chrysanthemums, carnations, dahlias and antirrhinums. Although the day she died was one of the saddest of my life, in a way I felt glad, because she was suffering. It wasn't unexpected, so it didn't come as a great shock. She had a great life, especially the last years of her life, because she was here.*

*In the main bedroom in London, which is decorated in Biedermeier style, Elton's striking bed stands in front of a mirrored wall topped by carved, gilded eagles holding up swags of muslin. Ravishing arrangements of pale-mauve hyacinths, cream 'Profita' roses and blush-white lilac are placed on the bedside tables. The walls and vast, concealed, clothes cupboards are softened by a gentle, duck-egg-blue-and fawn-striped fabric. Between the tall French windows which look over the courtyard garden, a bronze statue proudly stands on a burrwood plinth.*

A favourite mirrored-glass vase of Elton's, which always used to sit on his bedside table, is filled with golden yellow primulas.

A profusion of ravishing, peach-coloured roses and salmon-hued dahlias nestle together.

A mass of sunny daffodils in the garden dance in the spring breeze.

# Pink & Pale

For I am a mirror
I can reflect the moon.
I will write songs for you.
I'll be your silver spoon.

'GOODBYE' — MUSIC BY ELTON JOHN,

LYRICS BY TAUPIN.

*Musical notes, made out of rununculas of varying shades of pink, dance across a satin background, as if they had stepped off one of Elton's music sheets.*

*I love all roses, but especially yellow roses,*

*because they symbolize love and friendship.*

ELTON JOHN.

*Y*ears of tangled love affairs had Elton despairing of ever enjoying a stable personal life: 'As soon as anyone tries to find out about me, or to get to know me, I turn off. I'm afraid of getting hurt. I was hurt so much as a kid,' he once said. Now the man who has admitted that he 'took hostages' rather than forming relationships has found happiness and commitment with thirty-four-year-old David Furnish, a youthful, good-looking Canadian-born writer and film-maker. They met at one of Elton's dinner parties. Elton recently explained in an interview with Tony Parsons:

*Its something I've always wanted – to be loved and to have a really wonderful, close relationship with someone. I'm good at giving love but not at receiving it. And I am very good at entering into someone else's world but I always put up barrier when someone tries to enter into my world. I want the physical tenderness and affection, but there is a part of me that I have created that wants to push it away. David and I have been together for quite a while now and for him to give me a lot of love, which he does, is very difficult for me.*

'O Love, the very perfume of the rose.' This line from a poem by Hafiz, the fourteenth-century Persian poet, would seem to embody two essentials close to Elton's heart, as he told me:

*An imposing, nineteenth-century, bronze bust of Napoleon guards the entrance to Elton's London house. An extravagant arrangement on an antique Biedermeier console table greets visitors below his benevolent gaze. Plump peonies, deep-lilac delphinium, gerbera 'Lynx' and 'Delila' roses, together with pink antirrhinum and lisianthus, nestle among sprigs of copper beech. Further down the hall hangs a dramatically dark portrait of a gentleman painted by Balthazar Gerbier (1593–1667).*

*I am totally and utterly romantic and sentimental and I'm also a terrible schmaltz. So is David. We are very much alike in lots of ways, although I think my brain probably races a bit quicker than his. We remember every Saturday – as we met on that day – to give each other a card, writing down what has happened during the week. I don't give him flowers while we're here because I think it's a waste as the house is always full of them, but when we're away I always send him flowers. I think flowers are the most beautiful things to send to someone. They are very special. Even if it is a bunch of carnations with baby's breath in it, it's still better than getting a bunch of grapes.*

Elton's fabled generosity as a giver of presents is another facet of a man whose friends and family consider him one of the kindest people they know: 'When I send flowers I always send roses or a white orchid. I never send an arrangement if I can help it. An orchid will last and you can't go wrong with roses – the poet Robert Browning thought of the rose as "This glory garland round my soul",' Elton says. The gesture is often returned:

*Of course, I love receiving flowers too. I remember when I was ill in hospital in Australia having two growths taken out of my throat, George Michael, who is a dear friend, sent me this absolutely huge basket of red roses which lasted for ages. I had them by my bed and they were quite beautiful. I will always remember that. Gianni and Donatella Versace are also big flower-senders. They come by the lorry load in an incredible assortment of bunched loose flowers.*

Elton values his friendships, and was sufficiently moved by the death from AIDS of Freddie Mercury, of the rock band Queen, that his floral tribute of a hundred pink roses bore a card saying simply 'Thanks for being my friend: I will love you always'. George Michael, with whom Elton famously dueted on 'Don't Let the Sun Go Down On Me' at the Live Aid concert, is one of his younger comrades in the business. He has revered Elton since his adolescence, when he bought every album of Elton's as soon as it was released.

*Hot pinks and lush crimsons – gerberas, roses and peonies – against a dark background, combine with the intricately patterned, Versace bone china and the claret-coloured Venetian glass, to produce an effect reminiscent of a Dutch old-master painting.*

George is a great guy. He's got one of the best voices. Having always been fans of each other, we have a mutual appreciation society going – he's one of the most honest people I know, and going out to dinner with him is great value for money. He'll never hold back on anything and that's one of the reasons why I like him. He's very opinionated. The older I get, the more I appreciate that. I can't stand people who say 'I love this, I love that' and simply don't mean it.

Sting and his wife Trudie are also two of my best friends – he and I sing at a Rainforest concert each year in New York, although I no longer have many friends in the business. Kiki Dee – I don't see her very much – but she's a good friend. Theo Fennell [of the fashionable London jewellery store] and his wife Louise are two dear, kind friends. Right now, I buy more of Theo's stuff than

A multitude of complementary pinks spills over onto a nineteenth-century Biedermeier dressing table in Elton's London bedroom. A photograph of Brian, Elton's border terrier, who has fathered many of his ten dogs, takes pride of place beneath the blush-pink 'Sarah Bernhardt' peonies, roses, hanging love-lies-bleeding, lisianthus, cerise tulips and pale-pink phlox. Next to a photograph of himself in a gold-and-magenta, heart-shaped frame from Asprey's, lie Elton's two burrwood hairbrushes.

*A pair of black-alabaster leopard ornaments in the antique style prowl on a Biedermeier table in Elton's London bedroom beneath a profusion of 'Stargazer' lilies, gerberas, cerise antirrhinums, red cotonis and 'Chamilla' and 'Delila' roses.*

*anyone else's. One of the reasons why I adore him is because he is so innovative and creative, always trying different things. I'm also very fond of the boys from Take That – Gary Barlow and Robbie Williams.*

As well as buying Versace, also by the lorry load, the tunesmith and tailor have become close:

*Gianni has become one of my dearest friends. He's very similar to me, and has turned me on to so many different things, like neoclassicism and gardens, while I have introduced him to glass. I can't remember how long ago we met, but the more we saw of each other, the closer we became. Because I loved his clothes, I asked him to design special things for me. He did the staging and the album cover as well as the clothes for The One tour. Perhaps we have become especially close because he himself had an illness and has lately come increasingly out of his shell.*

*Pastel-coloured sweet peas in sugar-pink and frosted-whites hues bring an airy freshness to a bedroom. Behind the tissue-thin petals lies a Biedermeier chaise longue, covered in cool white satin silk.*

Elton works hard at contradicting the reasoning behind Georgia O'Keeffe's line: '…in a way nobody sees a flower, really, it is so small, we haven't time, and to see takes time, like to have a friend takes time.'

In 1995 Elton gave his partner the ultimate token of trust: by letting David follow him for one year with a video camera he has allowed him to film a frank and revealing diary of their life, a particularly painful process for Elton, who has an ingrained horror of taping videos. As he explains in the documentary:

*I'm not one for visual things. I don't like doing videos. I don't like my photo being taken. It's probably because of the way I look, the way I think I look, and the way I wish I looked. I'm not Madonna. I'm not someone who has a very strong visual image, so I don't feel that comfortable.*

Elton continues along this track during our talk:

*Emperors of the Tang dynasty in China (AD 618–906) exchanged and even offered peonies as marriage dowries. These luscious blooms were considered the kings of flowers, and often appeared alongside a phoenix, the king of birds, in paintings and pottery. Here a bowl of pale and medium-pink peonies, draped with French-organdie curtains caught with an antique, gilt-flower tieback, rests on a marble step.*

*If I am on 'Top of the Pops' I don't watch because I can't bear looking at myself. The reason I did the video was simply because I have been asked to do one so many times. So often when watching documentaries you don't actually find out about the person. It would have been impossible for David to do a documentary on me five years ago because I would have been totally out of it, and would have told David to bugger off within the first hour. But now I'm nearly fifty. I just think as you get older you have less tolerance for bullshit. I just said to David: 'Listen, I don't care how badly I come out of it. I don't want the documentary to be holier than thou, I just want people to see how I am and to know what actually goes on – the pressure, the bad behaviour, the good behaviour, the relationships – whatever happens in a year of touring.' Whenever he really cornered me, I didn't feel badly about it because it was David and I*

had that trust. After a while I didn't even notice the little camera. It was very like going through a year of therapy and here it is on film. Funnily enough, he was saying 'could you watch it?', and I told him 'It's the first thing on me, about me, that I could watch because I knew it was the truth, and I wasn't acting out a part.' I wasn't conscious of how I should be, how I should look. You know when you're pretending, and this had no pretences. This was the real macoy. I liked it, even though I sometimes thought God, I'm just like Zaza from 'La Cage aux Folles'! I watched it endlessly – we've both watched it so much that we could probably do a flawless stage version of it now!

*A burst of riotous colour, contrasting texture and form transforms a table. A combination of velvet-red 'Nicole' roses, cerise peonies, 'Ravel' roses, 'Lynx' gerbera and dark-red antirrhinums combine to produce an effect which is hot, rich and spirited.*

In the documentary 'Elton John: Tantrums and Tiaras' there are scenes in which Elton is convulsed with laughter by the irreverent repartee of Bob

*A small bunch of 'Delila' and 'Valerie' roses is a perfect complement to the pretty objects on the dressing table in a very feminine bedroom in Elton's country house. A nineteenth-century, Venetian toilette mirror on the dressing table catches the light which pours into a guestroom. The Victorian mother-of-pearl calling-card case, the dainty, nineteenth-century French opera glasses and the small Limoges boxes are reflected in the glass top. On the right lie a hand mirror and clothes brush, part of an Art Deco dressing-table set of pale-green, guilloche enamel.*

Halley. When asked if he thought Elton's music would continue to sell, Bob retorted: 'Nah. Load of old crap ain't it.' 'I think Bob steals the show really', Elton laughs.

> *That sort of bantering goes on between us all the time, through the good and the bad times. We've been together since our twenties, and he's got the greatest sense of humour which is absolutely lethal towards me. It's a bit like the film 'The Dresser' with Albert Finney and Tom Courtenay, a most magical picture in an old-fashioned way, expressing the sensibilities of a different era. But that's how Bob and I lived our lives. When we saw that film together, I said to him 'That's us. The only difference is that I will leave you something in my will!'*

*An enchantingly simple posy of pink autumn anemones, lilac scabious, mauve phlox, mint and majoram sits on a George I, walnut, bachelor's chest. The arrangement adds a further feminine touch to the Cinderella Room, and leads the eye to the central spray of roses within a band of roses, ribbon bows and pink scrollwork painted onto the large, Limoges, porcelain bombe table box. Scattered around the top of the chest are various other small, Limoges boxes.*

*So sweet a kiss the golden sun gives not*
*To those fresh morning drops upon the rose.*

WILLIAM SHAKESPEARE.

*The velvety petals of deep-crimson 'Ecstasy'*
*and wine-velvet 'Nicole' roses glisten with*
*drops from a burst of summer rain. As a*
*contrast to the rounded shapes and the 'Nicole'*
*roses' outer shade of white, the dramatically*
*coloured, spiky petals of the dark-red and cerise*
*dahlias nestle between the open blooms.*

Communication between lovers and close friends frequently involves floral messages. In the eighteenth century the oriental concept of the language of flowers caught the fancy of European sensibilities – until then floral symbolism had depended solely on the romantic and sentimental qualities of each flower: roses for love and daisies for innocence, pansies for thought, amaryllis for timidity and columbine for folly (as it resembled a jester's cap and bells). Letters penned by Lady Mary Wortley Montagu, writer, artist and wife of the ambassador to

Constantinople flowed from Turkey in 1718, filled with secrets gleaned from the harems: 'there is no colour, no flower, no weed, no fruit, herb, pebble or feather that has not a verse belonging to it; and you may quarrel, reproach, or send letters of passion, friendship or civility, or even of news, without inking your fingers'. During the sentimental age of the Victorians, when all manner of flowers flourished in the decorative arts, it became highly fashionable to give flowers in the form of jewellery as extravagant tokens of love and affection. Although Elton and David's jewelled gifts to each other are understandably more manly than flowery, Elton's passion for jewellery revolves around all things glittery from Versace, Theo Fennell, and Cartier. He first visited Cartier in 1971 with his close friend Nanette Newman, from whom his elevated taste in paintings and antiques was acquired when he asked her and her husband, Bryan Forbes: 'How can I learn "taste"?'

The days when Elton chose to dress outrageously, when his fans demanded a

spectacle on stage which he more than fulfilled, are long gone. 'I don't really feel the part until I'm into what I'm going to wear', Elton stressed more than once. 'I like a bit of outrage.' The crazy, rock-glitter stage outfits – winged Mr Freedom boots, feathered space-cowboy ensembles and wobbly, eight-inch-heeled platforms, fantastic plumage in the form of Mozart wigs and Eiffel Tower hats, angel wings and huge, spectacular glasses in the shape of the name ELTON – have been banished to a special building on the country estate next to a castle-style barn where his donkey lives, and are no longer

*The rich, maghogany, wooden panelling in a bathroom in Elton's country house is perfectly complemented by the elegant, striped-green wallpaper. Clusters of pink, claret and crimson madder anemones in coloured water are bunched together like a maharajah's rubies. The universal anemone, or the Greeks' favoured 'daughter of the wind', comes from their word* anemos, *meaning wind. A legend holds that the flower first sprang up at the foot of the cross from the blood of Christ .*

allowed to be photographed. Sartorial elegance on stage is now confined to trendy designer outfits – Versace's tomato-red PVC or black-and-white harlequin-patterned suits, complete with Italian shoes and a diamond stud in his right ear.

Since his rise to fame Elton has adored clothes and, having successfully escaped the lure of all his old, unhealthy pleasures, his one remaining addiction is his passion for acquiring them. Off stage, camp glamour still appeals to him, and he occasionally finds plundering the female wardrobe too tempting to resist – in the evenings he is not averse to dressing up in one of Versace's slinky, metal-mesh and lace dresses. Comic to some, outrageous to others, but Elton nevertheless manages to escape serious flack when 'frock-star' photos find their way into print. Not so a member of the royal family, famously short on fashion sense, whose appearance at a wedding provoked Nancy Mitford's comment: 'Unspeakable, like a hedgehog all in primroses.' Elton's tendency to swoop down on a shop and buy in bulk stems from his days in Pinner, as he explained to his biographer, Philip Norman: 'I still do it at incredible speed. It's all a hangover from childhood, when my mum would bring me up to London to look at a coat she wanted to buy. "I don't know," she'd always say. "We'd better come back next week and have another look."'

*The sumptuous colours in this bedroom are set off magnificently by the rich, mahogany wood in the nineteenth-century, French, walnut half-tester bed, which is enclosed by a dramatic, claret, fringed, paisley-tartan bedspread, and whose curtains are held in place by heavy, tasselled tiebacks. Various ruby- and wine-coloured velvet cushions rest on the paisley bedspread. A silver vase, holding deep-cerise and burnt-orange tulips sits on the round, early nineteenth-century, rosewood bedside cupboard, while on the other side can be seen a photograph of Elton with his late friend John Lennon.*

'Home is where one starts', according to T S Eliot. Being as devoted to his own home as a homing pigeon, Elton finds that one way of fighting the isolating effects of fame is by taking his closet – which contains amongst the creations of other designers, a vast amount of his favourite Versace silk shirts, jackets and suits, plus enough shoes to leave Imelda Marcos playing 'The Barefoot Contessa' – with him when travelling:

> *As I tend to get homesick, I do need my comforts, I need my home. If I am away from England for a year or so, I just really have to have my home on the road – then I don't feel so bad about hotels, however luxurious they are. As I said in David's documentary, I take so much because I never know what to wear and I like to have a choice. Wherever we go this is like my closet at home, so I feel like I am there, partly because travelling is so unbelievably boring. People think you are crazy – I suppose it is crazy, but it does keep me sane.*

Mountains of prescription sunglasses and other glasses follow him wherever he goes. These are placed in colour-coded drawers similar to those at home – pink, blue, purple and burgundy frames, green, red, silver, gold and black frames. And an indispensable part of the entourage are a couple of tiaras when travelling, 'because you never know when you're going to be invited to something formal'.

> *I'm hardly ever given flowers at concerts here. They are thrown on stage really only in Russia and America – mostly roses. I suppose it is a bit of a drag to go to a concert holding a bunch of flowers and then find the right moment to throw it.*

*A charming, nineteenth-century clock sits beneath the shadow of deep-cerise and burnt-orange tulips in a silver vase. The black-metal bedside lamps on marble bases boast griffin handles.*

*Six marble busts, bought from a palace in Buenos Aires, each in the form of a medieval emperor, stand guard in the hall leading to Elton's private apartments in his country house. They are adorned with two rows of pale-pink and white cymbidium orchids.*

Elton John was the first major Western rock star to perform in the former Soviet Union.

*I like very sad songs of any kind. I love things that make me weep – music, books, films, things that touch your soul. I've always found that both church music and beautiful classical music, as well as various popular songs, touch me. At the time when I was doing a lot of drugs I used to listen to 'Don't Give Up' by Peter Gabriel and Kate Bush, which kind of summed up my life. I used to weep openly over it. Also another song, Bruce Hornsby's 'Lost Soul', which again made me cry because it was exactly how I was in those days – always telling myself 'Yes, I will get better'. Those were days of very self-indulgent tears. But other music and songs, like Elgar's 'Enigma Variations', or Verdi's 'Requiem' and 'Abide With Me' and I'm off.*

As the man who sung 'Sad Songs (Say So Much)', perhaps his love of melancholy music stems from a nostalgia for something he has never found, similar to the locked emotions expressed in Wordsworth's wistful lament:

*To me the meanest flower that blows can give,*
*thoughts that do often lie too deep for tears.*

When it comes to writing his own music, Elton has the unique ability to complete a song as quickly as a swallow wings its way back to its nest at twilight. Until Bernie Taupin, his writing partner, went to live in Los Angeles, their working habits were an unusual blueprint for success. Both operated in

separate rooms, Bernie providing Elton with sheaves of his sensitive, polished lyrics for Elton to create music to the songs. Music trips off his pen in a steady stream:

> *It seldom takes me more than an hour to write a song. If the melody doesn't come to me I usually abandon it. I look at Bernie's lyrics to decide whether it's going to be a fast, slow or medium-paced song. Then I sit down at the piano and write a melody. I think I'm a good – a great – melody writer. I wish I could write my own lyrics, but I can't.*

In David's documentary, Elton's friend, the singer Lulu, expressed her somewhat incredulous admiration for his amazing song-writing methods: 'First you have a lyric. Then you write a tune round it. No-one else can do this but you.' David exclaims of his partner: 'I think he is a genius. It completely does my head in. Elton doesn't have a favourite song but I personally love 'Someone saved my life tonight'.

The variety of Elton's songs is infinite – sensitive and sympathetic, raunchy, romantic and rocking. As well as enjoying newer ballads in the vein of 'Sacrifice' and 'Nikita', along with the pulsating 'The Club at the End of the Street', his legion of fans remain faithful to many of his older songs – the ballad 'Your Song', his longest-living success; 'Daniel', a beautiful rendition of brotherly love; the poignant 'Candle in the Wind', a requiem for Marilyn Monroe which Elton wrote in half an hour, and the raucous rocker, 'Saturday Night's Alright For Fighting'. Twenty-three years ago Elton founded his own record label, the Rocket Record company, which releases his own albums as well as those of other popstar wannabes. With an encyclopedic knowledge of current music,

*A white-marble, nineteenth-century bust of a youth imitates Elton's contemporary look, as he sports a pink-carnation bow tie and Elton's famous boater, used in the video for 'I'm Still Standing'. Behind him can be glimpsed a boating picture,* Flirtation *(1885), by George Croegaert.*

he maintains an enthusiastic interest in the presently pulsating British pop-music renaissance. One of his latest collaborations was a melodic duet with Luciano Pavarotti, entitled 'Live Like Horses'.

*It was great working with him. I had tried to record the song previously and it just hadn't worked, so I kept it in a drawer. I had met Pavarotti one year doing the Rainforest concert with Sting, and suggested the idea to him. Eventually our schedules coincided. It's not a commercial record, but it's fun to put out separate singles and do a one-off song like that. I love it.*

Not being a man who relishes having idle time on his hands, Elton has also recently written a stage-musical version of *Aida* for Disney with Tim Rice. 'I really enjoyed doing that. On another level though, for me Jessye Norman is the definitive Aida', he says admiringly of the great American soprano.

As a young man, Elton began his career in the music business as an anonymous part of the British beat and blues scene in the mid-1960s, before being introduced to Bernie, then an equally unknown lyricist. Together they launched Elton's meteoric rise to fame. By 1972, having been swiftly catapulted onto the stages of the world's rock stadia, where he gradually lost his inherent shyness at the piano, the dynamic performer soon became America's favourite rockstar. So manic was his keyboard-bashing as he stood at the piano, that his fingers often bled. By the following year Elton was the biggest rockstar in the world, reaching the dizzy pinnacle of his glory years in the emotional 1974 Thanksgiving concert at Madison Square Garden, in which he sung a number of songs with his friend John Lennon. During that decade his music cut a wide swathe – seducing countless music fans from

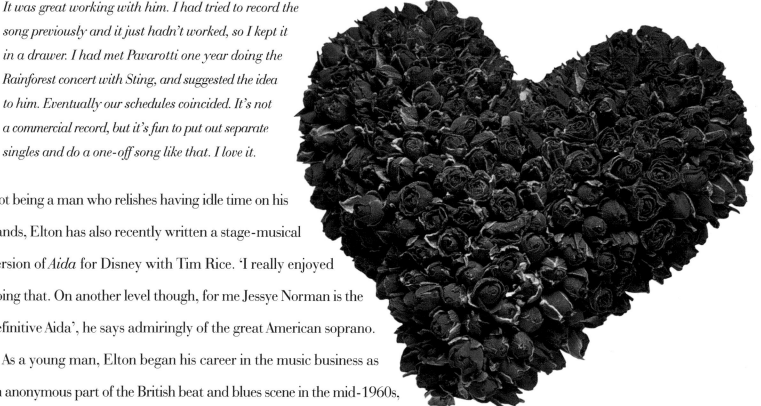

*A heart made of tiny, dried, pink miniature roses, backed by crimson velvet, is a perfect gift between lovers.*

*A plump cushion of soft-mauve and pink hydrangeas.*

hard-rock devotees to those who preferred their pop music on the easy-listening side.

Although he has said that being on stage is 'the only place I feel safe', twenty-five years of demanding tours and riding high in the charts take their toll. Readily admitting 'I am passionate about my work and actually like working for a living', even a megastar who takes a multitude of vitamins, bottles of English HP sauce and Marks and Spencer muffins ('because they are nice and healthy'), on tour, frequently finds life on the road tortuous: 'They just kill you, they physically kill you,' he has complained of his tours. 'I get very homesick and tired sometimes, and can't wait to go home. Of course I feel trapped by it all sometimes, but I love it.' He is only now just beginning to believe his audiences' wild enthusiasm at his concerts.

*'Audiences have always been very kind and generous to me. I was always embarrassed by it, and I suppose I just didn't trust their affection. I didn't know how to respond or how to accept praise. But I have begun to crack the audience thing, although I am still not great with personal compliments. All this stuff about how you have to love yourself – that's a hard thing to do.*

Few things distress Elton more on tour than to be greeted in his hotel room by an assortment of his least favourite flowers stuck randomly into a bowl.

*Flower-arranging should always be done in a vase but never in oasis, which is just a complete anathema to me. Flowers are given absolutely no chance to bloom and shine done that way. People who teach others to arrange flowers like that should be shot. There are certain things I absolutely refuse to have in my dressing room, especially chrysanthemums. I have either roses or lilies.*

# Kaleidoscope

Look up in the sky and tell me why
You're changing the colours before my eyes
Yellow blue green and blue
Settling on the window pane ...
... Still I sat beside the fire and watched it as it fell
Running colours from above into my citadel
My eyes are all embroidered
with the rainbows you have made
And now it seems just like strange rain.

'JUST LIKE STRANGE RAIN'

– MUSIC BY ELTON JOHN, LYRICS BY TAUPIN.

*Elton has a passion for all things Versace, who is a personal friend, be it suits, shirts, jewellery, bathrobes or china. His homes are filled with the brightly patterned clothes and objects which are the designer's hallmark. A blaze of colour from a random selection of Elton's silk shirts surrounds the flower arrangement. Various roses, delphinium, ginger, orange gerbera, cerise-pink antirrhinum, lisianthus, blue agapanthus and mauve gladioli form the majority of the flowers which burst like a multicoloured phoenix from a pinnacle of silk Versace scarves.*

*I love nooks and crannies in gardens. Rosemary Verey designed two English cottage gardens at Woodside, one of which has a porcelain pathway. They are very magical and special places for me. She placed two seats in them and I love to sit there, contemplating in the summer time, surrounded by huge hollyhocks, globe thistles and drifts of forget-me-nots and violas.*

ELTON JOHN.

To Elton, his eighteenth-century garden and woodlands constitute his own pocket of paradise – a word derived from the ancient Persian, meaning a garden or park – a green place. Throughout the ages various cultures believed that a cornucopia of flowers grew in paradise. Persians, like the Egyptians three thousand years ago, were famed for the beauty of their gardens, in particular their roses, and our delight in the scent of flowers stems from their essential oils, or attars, another beguiling word from the orient. These oils and fragrant perfumes were beloved by the Romans, who used the attar of roses, quinces and almonds in abundance when bathing.

Whatever new enthusiasm Elton embraces, he throws himself into it without reservation – one of his strongest characteristics:

*Gardens are things in which you are always planning ahead. Apart from a few trees, this garden is only six years old. When I had the house redone, we flattened everything and basically started again. You have to be very, very patient. It'll take a long time for it to grow and evolve, but one of the joys of having a new garden like this is that every year you see it blossom; it grows fuller and you can watch things mature. But if you plant new things each year,*

*A pair of massive, late nineteenth-century, Sèvres-style jardinières flank the hall door, which opens into the drawing room. Gilt rams' heads stand out amid the puce, blue and richly gilded trellissed body of each urn which sits on copies of Georgian stands created by Elton's woodcarver, John Biles. A kaleidoscope of colours fills each jardinière to the brim, including bright-yellow sunflowers and antirrhinum, lilac-coloured delphinium, blue hydrangea, 'Delila' and 'Renata' roses and rosy-red lisianthus.*

*you are bound to lose a certain amount. If you lose a tree it's like losing a kid.*
*It makes me sad because I feel trees represent ancient wisdom – they see*
*everything. We probably spend more money because of the trees than anything*
*else, but it is so beautiful to plant things like my favourite oaks, as well as*
*weeping willows, magnolias and the big catalpa – an Indian bean tree – on*
*the front lawn, and to watch things grow and prosper.*

*The flowers come forth like belles of the day.*

THOMAS JEFFERSON.

*Dappled light plays on a medley of colour made up of golden marigolds and scarlet salvias against a curtain of roses in a corner of the garden.*

As the learned and passionate lover of flowers, Eleanour Sinclair Rohde declared: 'We look down upon the flowers in our gardens, but they looked up to behold the beauty of the trees.' The English, who have infinitely more ancient oaks than any other country in western Europe – some living for well over 500 years – revere these venerable sylvan monuments. When a number of old oaks were recently felled in Windsor Great Park, one outraged critic compared it 'to chopping down the Queen Mother'.

When discussing whether flowers had soothed him during his troubled past, Elton's air of smiling self-mockery vanished and he became almost brutally honest:

*I had them around, but until I became sober my eyes didn't really clear. One's vision is so blurred. You think you are in control but you don't really know what you are doing. If you take drugs, and if you drink a great deal, you're not very finely tuned and you don't appreciate the natural, beautiful things that surround you. Your mind is completely on another track. Now I see so much more clearly. I notice things. I would never have walked round the garden before. Now I love it. The nice thing now is that I get up at seven o'clock in the morning, I see the sun rise, and notice how beautiful sometimes it is here first thing in the morning; how peaceful the cows look in the fields in the summertime. I would have tried to block out the daylight before. So my life in the last six years has been absolutely idyllic, having this house, this garden, and getting myself together.*

These days he is obviously a man in thrall to Arcadian pleasures, having found his way back through therapy, will-power and intense self-examination. His wistful song 'Skyline Pigeon', first released in 1968, epitomizes his new-found contentment:

> *Just let me wake up in the morning*
> *To the smell of new-mown hay;*
> *To laugh and cry; to live and die,*
> *In the brightness of my day.*

Many of the flowering plants that we take entirely for granted in English gardens began their existence in far-off lands where the art of horticulture had already been highly developed by their own, ancient civilisations. The Middle Kingdom in China was known as the flowery kingdom, and Confucius wrote of roses and orchids growing in China's Imperial Gardens as long ago as 500 BC. Each century has added to England's wealth of flowers, starting with the peripatetic Roman and Phoenician armies, who brought the rose and the Madonna lily with them as they travelled – the sweet-scented lily was used as a herb to heal the wounds of battle. The magnolia, amongst the

*Elton's Steinway grand piano is one of his most treasured possessions. Originally black, it has been so cleverly painted a faux walnut that the deception is barely detectable. A huge, swirling arrangement stands next to the piano. The rich, bonfire colours of autumn, together with the golden-brown piano draw the eye directly to this corner of the drawing room. Branches of deep-purple plums from the garden mingle with orange Chinese lanterns, red-maple and eucalyptus leaves, cerise cyclamen, peach dahlias and tiny browny-gold 'Singapore' orchids. Branches of spindleberry, with its tell-tale pink berries, and green leaves, can be seen placed among the brightly coloured flowers.*

*Not many musicians possess a piano stool whose carved and gilded legs end in the furry, cloven hooves of a goat. Appearing as if Elton has been momentarily interrupted in the midst of composing a new melody, a pair of his spectacles and the sheet music for his and Cliff Richard's score 'Slow Rivers Run Cold' lie on top of the green-grape-patterned damask covering.*

*In the country all of Elton's vegetables are organically grown. A harvest festival of freshly picked produce includes a giant pumpkin perching like a fattened sultan surrounded by his minions on a bench in the vegetable garden. Topped with a small thatch of red peppers, it looks as if it might have been overlooked at Hallowe'en picking. Succulent squashes, carrots, plump onions, wine-purple aubergines and radishes look tasty enough for a stealthy visit from Peter Rabbit.*

oldest flowering plants in the world, reached our shores from China and North America. Elton is so enamoured of white magnolias that 'when friends want to give me birthday and Christmas presents, I ask them for something to plant in the garden. Often I am given a small magnolia tree'.

During the sixteenth century, new plants were continuously being introduced into Europe by the powers who ruled the seas – the English, the Dutch and the Italians. The floodgates of China's floral wealth were flung open during the next two centuries, bringing us chrysanthemums, azaleas,

rhododendrons and camellias — a flowering plant which dates back to prehistoric days, and numbers of which form an enchanting glade near the ornamental lake in Elton's garden. An eighteenth-century white marble statue of Sir George Cook, much coveted by the Victoria and Albert Museum, has lately been added, and nestles like a pale moonstone amongst the camellias. And from South Africa came the agapanthus, freesia and pelargonium. Like a hummingbird returning to collect the nectar from his favourite blossom, Elton often revisits the treasured places in his garden:

*A feeling of peaceful harmony is apparent when stepping from the front hall into the expansive drawing room in Elton's country house. Four sets of French windows open onto a terrace where Elton entertains friends on summer evenings. The room is filled with superb antiques, paintings and objets d'art. The eye is immediately drawn to the imposing, seventeenth-century painting* Diane and Actaeon *by Alessandro Turchi on the furthest wall. It hangs above a highly polished, Regency, serpentine, bombe* commode *with an orange-and-green veined-marble top, above which sits an intricate, nineteenth-century, sandalwood and ivory box inset with silver. On the Regency card table in the foreground stands a profusion of roses, lilies, hydrangeas, lisianthus and antirrhinum, ranging from shell-pink to cerise in hue.*

*Down by the monkey tree near the Orangery we have just planted some Japanese maples. Having witnessed the most amazing autumn I have ever seen in Atlanta, the most richly beautiful of all the seasons I think, and seen how that red colour changes, I came home to Woodside and had an overwhelming urge to plant some. So that is another special nook I love.*

Celia Thaxter, the nineteenth-century writer and poet, lyrically describes an idyllic start to her day: 'When in these fresh mornings I go into my garden before anyone is awake, I go for the time being into perfect happiness … the fair face of every flower salutes me with a silent joy that fills me with infinite content.' Bucolic simplicity and individual imagination, do not, however, suffice for those daunted at the prospect of creating their own garden-paradise. Garden designers have become highly fashionable once again, with Rosemary Verey, famous for the work that she did for Prince Charles at Highgrove, leading the way as Britain's horticultural *grande dame*. In the eighteenth century, 'the age of improvement', Capability Brown, that most eminent of English landscape gardeners, whose real name was Lancelot, earned his nickname because he would ceaselessly deliberate upon the enormous 'capabilities' for the improvement of the gardens and grounds that he was asked by the doting gentry to landscape.

*A George III burr-yew tea caddy and nineteenth-century Mauchlin-ware snuffboxes nestle beneath a magnificent arangement. Beside the flowers on the matching card table behind the sofa, (below) a peach-coloured arrangement includes gerberas and dahlias, antirrhinum and lisianthus.*

Six years ago Rosemary Verey redesigned Elton's rolling, rococo garden, (from which one can see Windsor Castle with the flag flying if the queen is home) and he holds the spry septuagenarian in high esteem: 'Rosemary's a sensational woman. She's incredibly energetic, never stops, is always going on lecture tours … I don't know how she does it. She's just a wonderful creature. I adore her.' With the help of freelance designers Gordon Taylor and Guy Cooper, Rosemary Verey spent four years paying daily visits to Woodside to oversee the groundwork involved in laying out the foundations of the new garden – generous swathes of lawn punctuated by beech hedges, scented

*A Meissen china plate is filled with such exquisitely crafted blossoms that it seems hard to believe they have not been freshly picked from the garden. A medley of sapphire-blue gentians, small melons, fuchsia-pink roses, orange ranunculus and apple blossoms mix with other flowers on Elton's dining-room sideboard to continue the floral theme throughout the house.*

borders and an ornamental lake. Flower beds filled with a patchwork quilt of flowering plants were added, as well as a bold water feature, whose arching water jets were adapted from the famous fountain canal in Granada in southern Spain, which leads up to a wooden gazebo. Although fountains seem today to be an added luxury in our often modest-sized gardens, they were usually the dominating feature in all medieval and sixteenth-century gardens, however small. It was only in the seventeenth century that the fountain – with its life-giving, purifying water – was replaced by the sundial.

One of Rosemary Verey's first designs was the white garden, full of narcissi and daffodils that danced in the gusting March winds like a swarm of huge, white butterflies. The heavy scent of clusters of white hyacinths drifted through the

*This flashing, neon-lit 1960s Wurliberg jukebox, which has been fitted to contain sixty CDs, continually changes colour from mauve to green, from red through orange to yellow.*

*I'm blue tonight, I'm red when I'm mad I'm green when I'm jealous, yellow when I'm sad.*

'BETWEEN SEVENTEEN AND TWENTY' –
MUSIC BY ELTON JOHN, LYRICS BY TAUPIN.

*A stunning collection of vases in every colour and size consists of mainly antique Lalique and 1950s Venini Murano – Venetian art glass.*

*A massive urn filled with a profusion of sunflowers, raspberry 'Hercules' amaryllis, ginger, lilac, orange gerbera, 'Nicole', 'Ravel' and 'Sunrise' roses, magenta 'Serena' gerbera and 'Gelda' roses, arranged especially for a party, is touched by the morning sun.*

open windows into Elton's study. What had originally been an outdoor, five-a-side football pitch, trimmed with Watford Football Club logos, was now all symmetry and curving borders filled with tulips, spiraea and white-flowered lamium. Elton, a keen tennis player and fanatic outdoor-sports lover (he is the only rock star to have played both cricket at Lord's and tennis at Wimbledon) shared a passion for football with his father as a youngster, in particular for his local team Watford Football Club. Having once been Watford's chairman, he is currently its lifetime president, and admitted in an interview several years ago: 'The football club helped me through a really difficult time. It gave me something else to do rather than being Elton John all the time.'

Elsewhere in the garden, a long, herbaceous border was divided into five sections, each with its own colour scheme – the herbaceous border was invented by the Victorian gentry when the number of flowers planted in their garden's flower beds indicated the extent of their wealth. The most fabled white garden of all, of course, is the one at Sissinghurst Castle, designed and planted in the snowy winter of 1949 by Vita Sackville-West, who said: ' … I cannot help hoping that the great, ghostly barn-owl will sweep silently across a pale garden, next summer, in the twilight, the pale garden that I am now planting under the first flakes of snow'.

*The magnificent, eighteenth-century, circular, specimen marble table, with lion-paw feet, incorporates numerous rectangles of lapis-lazuli, malachite and porphyry segments. Standing in the middle of the Orangery, it is one of Elton's favourite situations for flower arrangements. A profusion of roses – orange 'Unique', crimson 'Nicole' and 'Ravel' entwine themselves with 'Serena' gerbera, 'Gelda' roses, orange euphorbia and blue lisianthus. On the far wall hangs Nicolas de Largillière's ravishing portrait of the Countess de Ruppelmonde (1707), one of a pair, in a sumptuous vermillion gown, who seems to look longingly out into the sun-drenched garden.*

But gardens, like oyster-grey storm clouds, continually change shape and direction before reaching their full potential. And so the white garden has been moved to make room for a more dramatic interpretation – Elton's creative imagination is forever on the move:

*I am always thinking ahead, have always got a project in mind. Gianni Versace is the same. He suggested I build a formal Italian garden with pavilions and statues. I asked Sir Roy Strong, who had designed Gianni's garden in Como, to do it, because of their friendship. I think if you meet artistic people, you know they have something to offer as soon as you do. People like Roy Strong and Rosemary Verey can teach you so many things. They have a world of experience in things you know little about. I have learnt so much from both of them.*

*The Italian garden was done very quickly, starting in January and finishing in April. The only logical place you could have it near the house, and at the same time reach into the field to get the right perspective, was where Rosemary had planted the beautiful white garden. It was a wrench, because I didn't want to get rid of her garden, so we shifted it over and now it will have to grow all over again. Already the white flowering roses, one of my all-time favourites, are flourishing. The Italian garden, with its mass of scarlet geraniums surrounded by boxwood, is very striking because you can go and look at the house from the avenue of trees leading to the obelisk, and the house looks better than it did before.*

The light and airy Orangery, which boasts five sets of French windows opening onto the garden, was totally gutted and redesigned six years ago. It was previously the home of Elton's grandmother. Now gilded and painted the palest duck-egg blue, with a ceiling mural featuring contemplative angels and roses, the main reception room is now the imposing home to a collection of exquisite furniture and fine paintings. A pair of eighteenth-century, satinwood, demi-lune tables in the style of Robert Adam each stand behind a pair of apple-green, Chippendale sofas, part of the George III Hercules suite. Vases of dark-blue lisianthus flowers flank the large sofa, above which hangs the important painting Le Poisson et Le Pêcheur (1730) by Jean Baptiste Oudry.

*The first glimpse of Woodside, which was originally built in the eighteenth century, as seen from the drive after entering the heavy, wrought-iron gates. The elegant house, basking in the morning sun, is reflected in the ornamental lake, which is surrounded by rolling lawns and a camillia glade. A row of small, pruned yew trees stand guard behind a nineteenth-century, marble statue acting as a sentry at the entrance to the property.*

(When the twelve-foot-high stone obelisk was erected, it was mistakenly reported in the press to be a thirty-foot statue of a penis.) Elton continued:

*When I look out of my bedroom window the view is far more striking. And now, of course, with all the plants and wild red poppies which have been put in the fields, it will grow and look more substantial in a few years.*

*The very first thing I do when I come back to Woodside after being away is to walk through the front hall all the way to the back door, have a look at the flowers and then walk all the way back through the house admiring them. I think Julia and Susie are geniuses when arranging flowers for me. They know exactly what I like, and the flowers are always beautiful. I would never think of putting certain coloured roses together, for instance, strong apricot and pale amethyst, but they do it brilliantly. It's also lovely in winter when they use branches and berries. And at Christmas-tree time we have fun using all the ornaments. Last year we had Tiffany balls and bells, as well as beautiful old ones that we found in Milan.*

*A small, apple-green, Victorian vase holds a simple arrangement of narcissi, grape hyacinths and intricate, check-patterned, snakeshead fritillaries.*

*I like both bright and subtle colours in flowers. Sometimes you can walk into the house and see something so vivid it's quite stunning. Then other arrangements are muted and pastel, which appeals to me. I think in a house like this you have to be careful. In the bathroom, for example, the girls have placed the most incredible anemones – the flower that means forsaken. I thought 'Wow, they look fantastic'. I love that. But they have never gone overboard.*

As many as one thousand flowers are used weekly for the country house, and 650 for London.

A further manifestation of Elton's pleasure in all things rural is pottering around his *jardin potager*, the entrance to which is flanked by two vast Mediterranean olive jars.

*My vegetable garden, in which everything is organically grown, is just fabulous. I love it. Everything is healthy and tastes better. And as for our pumpkin that won third prize in the south of England horticultural show, I've never seen a bigger pumpkin in my life – it weighed one hundred and seventy pounds. I was so proud. Before the great change six years ago we never grew a thing here. One of the problems was rabbits, and the other was not enough manpower – when you have a garden this size you have to have enough people caring for it, otherwise you can't make a go of it. Charlie, our head gardener, who has been with us for years, is very knowledgeable. We have five extremely good, full-time gardeners, which I think is absolutely necessary. We cut roses, gladioli, sweet peas, sweet-william, peonies, yellow daisies, dahlias and scabious from the potager and garden, which is lovely.*

*Julia and Susie in the flower room at Woodside. Working for their only client takes up most of their working week. It can take six hours to compile the weekly list of flowers for each room at both Woodside and Queensdale.*

# White & Cream

...This is my bed

This is where I sleep

That was the dark

Those are my dreams

They belong to me

'HOUSE'

MUSIC BY ELTON JOHN,

LYRICS BY TAUPIN.

A small, gold, piano brooch of Elton's sits on the soft lip of an arum lily.

*The greatest thing my success has brought me is the ability to look after my family and to improve their lives by making them more comfortable. Also being able to share what I've got. There is no point in having success and not being able to share it with the people who helped you. It is a team effort, and I suppose I'm like the leader of a big team. I'm a very good giver, but not such a good receiver.*

ELTON JOHN

*I*t is Elton's habit of sharing his rewards that has reaped dividends.

*The foxglove, with its bell-shaped head and connotations of woodland secrets, has always been associated with fairies, goblins and the 'little people'. A bunch of foxgloves and white 'Iceberg' roses, tied with a silk ribbon, lies across the invitingly feminine Victorian brass bed in a guestroom. Above the George I walnut, bachelor's chest hangs one of a set of four botanical paintings by Mrs Moivres (c. 1820). Below it rests a portrait of a female depicted as an artist by C R Bone. The following note was found sewn into the lining of a gown from which the beautiful cushions on the bed were made: 'This embroider'd Gown was worked by Elizabeth Periam it was begun in the year 1785 and finish'd in the year 1790. It is given to her Daughter Elizabeth Periam Hoods.'*

*That is why I have the people around who have stayed with me for so long, like John Reid, Bob Halley, Bob Stacey, Robert Key, John and Jenny Newman, Derek Baulcombe, Brenda Woodstock and all the others. They are part of my family. I love having them close and enjoy helping them. But you can't buy loyalty. I can't think of any other artist, and I know them all, with a more loyal group of people than I have. And I'm very proud of that.*

The superstar's entourage, which his partner has ingenuously compared to 'a medieval court', is infiltrated by ten dogs – seven border terriers, one mongrel and two Irish wolfhounds – to whom Elton is equally devoted:

*I think mutts can sometimes be far the most intelligent, loving and loyal of dogs. If there was a fire in the house, I would never grab a possession. I'd grab the dogs which I love so much. People and dogs are far more important than anything else. I get terribly sad when one of the dogs dies – it's just heartbreaking. I was told by my doctors when I came out of rehabilitation treatment six years ago that it would be good for me to live on my own and do things for myself. I had never lived on my own in my life. I had always lived with either my family, people who worked for me, or in relationships. So I rented*

*The chapel was built in memory of Elton's beloved nan, Ivy Sewell, who resided in the original, eighteenth-century Orangery before it was totally gutted and rebuilt. A feeling of peace and quiet pervades the entire building. Off the drawing room, wrought-iron grills open onto a small chapel which features gold-leafed, swan-necked pediments. On each pediment is*

*Elton's personal coat of arms, bearing the inscription 'Eltono es Bueno'. (See page 128 for details). The two extremely rare and valuable, seventeenth-century, giltwood chairs (of a set of only six in existence) originally resided in the private apartments of King William III at Hampton Court. They are covered in heavy crimson velvet and trimming.*

*Queensdale in London and immediately got Thomas from the Battersea Dogs Home and lived on my own for a year. He is just the most gorgeous dog, about nine years old, so friendly and a total lapdog. I would get up at six o'clock every morning, take Thomas for a walk and attend an AA meeting.*

Brian, a terrier, sits basking on Elton's knee as he talks, with all the confidence of one of the pampered Pekinese of the last dowager empress of China. 'Brian is one of my favourites. You're the daddy of most of the dogs roaming round here, aren't you?' asks Elton, kissing him affectionately. David Furnish has seen the effect on Elton of losing a pet: 'When one of his favourite dogs died the first person he called was his mum. She is always there for him.' Elton's dear, departed friends have their own headstones in a corner of the garden.

Thomas, a handsome, tan-and-black mutt, still lives at Queensdale, Elton's London home in leafy Holland Park, which was once an old

*And if my hands are stained forever*
*And the altar should refuse me*
*Would you let me in, would let me in,*
*Should I cry sanctuary.*

'THE KING MUST DIE'

– MUSIC BY ELTON JOHN, LYRICS BY TAUPIN.

*Light from the setting sun filters through a silhouette of trees and ivy, bringing a sense of tranquility to the delicate, grey-green cupola and carved-stone pillars of a restored, late eighteenth-century gazebo.*

cardboard factory. Tucked away in a cul-de-sac, the snug house is surrounded

by small, early nineteenth-century houses intended as servants' quarters for

the rich people who lived in the nearby squares. Once bought, it was totally

refurbished with the help and orchestration of his interior designers, Andrew

Protheroe and Adrian Cooper-Grigg, and currently reflects Elton's passion

for Biedermeier harmony. Most of the rooms are filled with nineteenth-

century Scandinavian and German Biedermeier furniture, while other pieces

were specially made by John Biles in a similar style to fit specific areas. A

feeling of cool, 1930s-inspired neoclassical calm and order has been

established, from the stone-and-marble inlaid flooring in the entrance hall,

to the cool trompe-l'oeil stonework and Elton's grand bed topped by carved

and gilt eagles. Splashes of exuberant colour from the imaginatively arranged

*An orderly avenue of grass and white flowers flanked by stately, Italian, eighteenth-century stone urns leads away from the Italian garden.*

*The seventh fine art – gardening, not horticulture, but the art of embellishing grounds by fancy.*

THOMAS JEFFERSON.

A valuable set of Sèvres-porcelain potpourri vases draped in leopard skins were originally bought to complement the large, important painting in the Orangery, Le Poisson et Le Pêcheur (1739), by Jean Baptiste Oudry. In the painting, a young fisherman lies upon the river bank, a leopard skin loosely covering his body.

vases of flowers in each room bring the house alive. 'When we've come back to Queensdale after being away and there haven't been any flowers there, it's completely dead. It's just not the same', laments Elton. Tall windows open out from the drawing room on to a paved courtyard garden, which is well stocked with potted plants.

*I think that each of my houses has a different feel. Woodside is very countrified. Queensdale is light and very comfortable with all the Biedermeier, while my new house at the top of the harbour in Nice in the south of France is going to be an eclectic mixture of stone, iron, glass, wood and marble – five textures together forming a mixture of incredible modern art. Julian Schnabel is making me a bed and I've bought two of his paintings, as well as a few Warhol/Basquiat collaborations and an Eric Fischel. Theo Fennell is making me a canteen of cutlery which in years to come will be revered as a beautiful antique. There will be a marble bath and classical marble Roman busts in the house, as well as classical paintings which I've recently bought. Basically, it will be totally white inside with the colour coming from the coloured glass. Typically, I've already furnished it before it's finished.*

An arrangement of moonlight-yellow 'Cappuccino' and creamy pink 'Emile' roses blend in with white peonies, cream delphiniums, double-cream lisianthus. and branches of white leaf .Country-style Chippendale chairs, part of a set of twelve in the dining room, rest beneath the brass urn, always considered to be merely a flower container, but once dropped on the floor, the ashes of a long-departed stranger were discovered.

However much Elton adores England, 'I also love France, and the more I go to Italy, the more I fall in love with it. I would like to get an apartment there which would be perfect for the winter.' A part of him also feels totally committed and comfortable on the other side of the Atlantic:

*America has been my second home for many years. I have received a lot of love and acceptance there. People like the fact that I've gone to their country and have said some nice things about Atlanta, because basically the people there, who are very friendly, have welcomed me with open arms. I really do like them, they are so polite, with lots of Southern charm, always saying 'Hi, how y'all doin'.*

David understands America's pull on Elton's loyalties: 'Atlanta is resolutely immune to celebrity culture. Elton can walk around a shopping mall or drive his car. It makes him feel normal. There's a side of his life in Atlanta which feeds his soul. It kind of balances him.' Elton agrees:

*In Atlanta I can do what I want, I can drive where I want. I don't have a driver. I drive myself and feel I fulfill a part of myself that I can't elsewhere. I really only drive in England when I go and see my mum. Also there I can do things for myself like go to the supermarket, which is extremely important because I lost all that when everyone did everything for me.*

Elton's Atlanta home combines five apartments with two duplexes high up on two floors of a building overlooking the city. 'As I started collecting photography, I had to buy the next apartment, so it gradually became bigger and bigger. The views are incredible. I have a number of

*Elton and his heraldic designers added a tongue-in-cheek touch when creating his personal coat of arms in the chapel. It is reproduced discreetly on four simple 'gold-leaf' swan-necked pediments high up around the tops of all the chapel's walls. Beneath a standard heraldic design the top part represents piano keys. The design below depicts Elton's gold discs. The motto Eltono es Bueno is a double entendre, expressing the message that not only is the music or song good, but also that Elton is good. The result is both endearing and an example of how, in his chapel, Elton cleverly manages to combine humour with an abiding affection for his departed nan, and his friends who have died of AIDS, which include the exceptionally talented Freddie Mercury, lead singer of the band Queen. Elton's floral tribute at the funeral of his close friend in November 1991 was simply one hundred roses. (Extra plaques with lists of friends are soon to be added to Chapel walls.)*

*One of Elton's most charming, porcelain* objets d'art *reminds one of a winged fairy king. An early Victorian (1840), Staffordshire porcelain figure, he is perhaps an allegorical representation of a Greek god. He appears deep in thought as he sits on a green foundation, his loins covered in a sepia-coloured cloth, writing a large tome with his plumed pen. A sprig of orange blossom from Elton's garden grows out of one of the twin wells of the pen-holder. On either side of his feet are two square recesses which were intended for use as inkwells.*

balconies which are quite beautifully landscaped with about sixteen thousand plants.'

Each of Elton's houses is filled with what he loves best: 'I love books. Books are precious. Books, music, flowers, paintings, furniture – I love all the prime, staple things of the arts that you can have in your home.' His books are bought principally at John Sandoe, a small, friendly eighteenth-century shop in London beloved by its clients, who return year after year. Elton pops in regularly whenever he is in town:

Heavy, mahogany doors with gilt door handles open on to Elton's private suite in his country house. A tranquil painting by Henry Scott Tuke (1858–1929) of a boy lying languidly on the beach gazes down on a gentle arrangement of hydrangeas, foxgloves, delphiniums, soft-cream and yellow roses and purple-flowering mint. A pair of early nineteenth-century, bronze mantel urns with yellow-grained marble bases are filled with potpourri. They stand on a superb George III, satinwood, demi-lune side table, the top of which is crossbanded with tulipwood, with its wide outer band featuring ribbon-tied swags and foliate roundels in various woods.

A mass of delicate, white sweet peas spills out of a tall, nineteenth-century, Meissen blue-and-white epergne in the Blue Room in the country. The intricately designed objet d'art is encrusted with floral decorations and eight male and female putti, including one warming his hands over a flame, and another with a wreath of grapes and goblet.

My favourite reads are invariably biographies – I like to find out about people and I like anything that is well-written. The best autobiography I've ever read were two volumes by the fabled classical concert pianist Arthur Rubenstein. I couldn't put it down. He wrote the second in his eighties and could remember everything – which girl he was dating in Montevideo in 1912. It was funny, witty and he was incredibly articulate. He came across as a really saucy sod, who loved fondling ladies under the table.

Elton may be a man of eclectic taste and many passions, but clearly religion is not a strong element in his life. He states sceptically when discussing his lack of faith:

I took myself a

blue canoe

And I floated

like a leaf

Dazzling,

dancing,

Half enchanted

In my Merlin

sleep.

'WHERE TO NOW
ST. PETER?'
– MUSIC BY
ELTON JOHN,
LYRICS BY TAUPIN.

*Comprising a romantic entwining of limbs and gentle caresses, this fine statue is one of a set of four by Luigi Grossi which stands inside the Orangery. The morning sunlight outlines the softly rounded marble contours of the pair of lovers, bought recently as Eros and Psyche.*

*I was brought up as a Protestant, and am not really religious at all in the conventional sense. I'm someone who believes in a god, or in a higher power, but I'm extremely distrustful of the way religion divides people. I dislike that side of it intensely – it makes me angry. I like the concept of religion, but I am not so sure about the way it is dealt with – the administration of it all. I sometimes think religion is just a money-making business which instils fear in people and unconsciously breeds a great deal of hatred.*

*Having said that though, I often go to the chapel that I built in memory of my nan in the Orangery. Every time I go in there I get the shivers. There's something special down there. Knowing that she was an old woman, one of the joys of having my grandmother living here was not having to worry about her being beaten up and stuff like that. When she died, I couldn't get back for the funeral as I was receiving my Oscar, so later I got the family together and we scattered her ashes amongst the flowers and said a little prayer for her in the garden.*

Flowers have been used as decoration in the ceremonies of every religion, but as they were often considered luxury objects by the Christian church they also served as powerful symbols for the vanity of human life and the transience of worldly riches. In the seventeenth century, the passing beauty of flowers was caught in the symbolic 'vanitas' still-life paintings, often depicted beside a human skull – a symbol of mortality – or a candle, denoting the fleeting nature of existence, as well as bottled potions, feathered quills, books and ripe fruit. These pictures, with their emblems of death, were painted to convey messages and to teach moral lessons. Flowers reminded people that since they bloomed and died as quickly a blossom, they should be mindful of the spiritual principles of Christianity and attempt to lead a pure life.

The Madonna lily, the epitome of purity and whiteness, was painted as a symbol of the Virgin Mary, as well as of Christ himself, while violets were

recognized as everyday symbols of piety, humility and the Christian faith.

Originally dismissed as a symbol of pagan Rome, the rose also came to play

a central role in the Christian religion. By the fifteenth century, its petals were

an emblem for the five wounds inflicted on Christ, and the blood spilt by the

early martyrs was represented by red roses. This much-loved beauty (beating

only the gladiolus as the world's most popular cut flower), also gave its name

to the glorious, stained-glass windows of cathedrals, as well as the rosary

*The delicate, ivory-white petals of a sprig of 'Phalaenopsis' orchid are opened fully to reveal a hint of the madder-rose and canary-yellow colours hidden deep inside.*

*If you gave her the world,*

*and it was covered in pearls*

*She'd only ask for the moon . . .*

'SNOW QUEEN' – MUSIC BY ELTON JOHN,

LYRICS BY TAUPIN.

which was once fashioned out of crushed rose

petals or rosehips, its poppy-red fruit.

Compassion for others is another strong element

of Elton's multifaceted make-up. He is mainly

responsible for rock music embracing the AIDS

*Shells have enchanted mankind since the beginning of time. The inventive beauty of shells is infinite, and in them we can see the 'housing' of creatures of the sea. When decoration reached a peak of extravagance and resplendence in the eighteenth century, fanciful shell grottos were created in the palaces, mansions and gardens of the European nobility, especially those of the frivolous and luxury-loving French. Situated in the shell-and-coral grotto of Elton's country house, this charming dolphin is the proud possessor of scalloped fins and a helmet-shell mouth. Surrounded by 'Phalaenopsis' orchid blossoms, filigree strands of smilex and pearl-white shell flowers, he gazes serenely down upon his bounty of pearls and orchids that cascade from a giant clam.*

catastrophe, cutting charity records and giving fund-raising concerts to help

to try to find a cure for its sufferers. 'When I announced I was gay in 1976, a

lot of radio stations in the US stopped playing my records', Elton has said on

more than one occasion. Having selflessly performed for charities and good

causes for the past twenty years, he eventually set up his own Elton John

AIDS Foundation. He discussed his thoughts in David's documentary:

*The French windows of the dining room open on to a stone verandah (designed by Guy Cooper and Gordon Taylor) with a pond holding six red, white and orange koi carp. A water canal featuring arching water jets has been created to add a continuous vista from the house – an adaptation of the famous fountain canal in Granada, Spain. At the end of the canal, near a large willow, stands a copper-roofed wooden gazebo, which encloses a yellow-leafed catalpa, a form of Indian bean tree, while Irish yews guard the gazebo like protective sentries.*

*When it comes to my sexuality, living a lie is not worth it. You only get one attempt on this earth, and it is so much better to be yourself. When you do a concert for the foundation it is so much more pleasurable than a normal concert, because you know you are raising a lot of money for a really good cause.*

*I've lost quite a few people this year – people I really loved a lot, including Mark, a dear friend who worked for the band and was someone whom I've known for seven years. He was only twenty-four and was the sweetest boy. Once he got ill he never had another chance. Even though we expected him to die in a couple*

A simple bowl of Elton's favourite 'Renata' yellow roses, cream lisianthus and ranunculus welcome him to his London kitchen. Placed between the shelves that hold Chinese blue-and-white jars and vases, a profusion of jasmine, stephanotis, 'Casablanca' lilies and 'Phalaenopsis' orchids add a delicate fragrance to the morning air that wafts in from the small, plant-filled garden. A colourful painting titled Crisis: Still Life with Flowers and Fruit by Sir Cedric Morris (1880–1982) adds an eye-catching touch to the

*The church bells ring out morning glory When summer bends to the winter's rage.*

'EMILY'
– MUSIC BY
ELTON JOHN,
LYRICS BY
TAUPIN.

of weeks, it just shook me. I've really stopped counting all the friends who have died of AIDS this year. I think politicians who say AIDS isn't really a problem are misinformed. I think they're bigoted and their anger is homophobic. Bigots will be bigots, and they will always attack the people they hate the most. So it doesn't surprise me.

Elton returns to the subject while sipping a diet Coke at Woodside:

*Recently I was part of a wonderful occasion in the Riverside Chapel in New York with Jessye Norman for her AIDS benefit which educates black people about the disease through the church. Jessye came up the aisle leading the gospel choir in robes and then sang the most beautiful spiritual song. There was Whoopi Goldberg, Maya Angelou, Toni Morrison, Bill Jones, the dancer, Max Roach, the jazz drummer, the choir and myself. I was the only white boy there, and I sang 'Border Song'. At one point Whoopi said 'I want you all to get up and tell us the name of someone whom you have lost through AIDS, and it was like a*

A nineteenth-century statue in the antique style stands in the wintery garden in front of a row of weeping cherry trees.

*Of all the flowers
in the mead
Then love I most those
flowers, white and red,
Such as men call daisies
in our town.*

GEOFFREY
CHAUCER.

*A charming bronze statue
which once belonged to
the ballet dancer Rudolf
Nureyev clicks his
castanets as he dances
with a daisy chain
draped around his hand.*

*cleansing. We all got up and there was a continual buzz for five minutes. It was extraordinary – the music, the atmosphere, and Jessye's singing. She is amazing – for me one of the most beautiful women on the planet, like a galleon. She's like no other.*

When I asked Elton if he considered himself to have finally found a measure of happiness, he replied:

*Oh yes, finally, although I've been through a lot in my fifty years. My life has been a rollercoaster ride of ups and downs – fantastic times, really depressing times, incredibly irresponsible times. I think it is essential to have fulfilment in life as far as personal relationships go, and now I'm very happy with that. But I don't think I was ever mature enough to get to the point where I was ready to have a personal relationship that would last until the last four or five years. Apart from enjoying my happiness and helping those less fortunate, I just want to continue composing music which appeals to others because that's what I really love doing.*

*Elton frequently takes a couple of tiaras with him when travelling, 'because you never know when you are going to be invited to something formal'. Here a simple tiara lies on a pretty floral cushion.*

*You're a cushion uncrumpled*

*You're a bed that's unruffled*

*And I believe in the snow queen*

*That's somewhere in the hills*

*She's got the world on a string.*

'SNOW QUEEN'

– MUSIC ELTON JOHN,

LYRICS BY TAUPIN.

Elton's song 'You Gotta Love Someone' says it all:

*You can cheat the devil and slice a piece of the sun*

*Burn up the highway but before you run*

*You gotta love someone*

*You gotta love someone.*

*While nature sleeps, the Italian garden, with its statues of musicians, balustrades and Italianate pavilions, remains all symmetry and order in the early morning sun. A swathe of lawn lined with birch trees stretches out to a stone obelisk topped with a gilded ball in the distance.*

*When the last of the summer roses fade in the garden here, I can look forward to a spectacular red-and-golden fall in America.*
ELTON JOHN.

# *T*hanks to:

ELTON JOHN

DAVID FURNISH

BOB STACEY
GEORGE,
JENNY,
LINDA,
LYN
CHARLIE AND
THE GARDENERS
MARK SUMMERFIELD
AND EVE FERRET
ANDREW PROTHEROE
&
ADRIAN COOPER-GRIGG
ANDREW ACQUIER
STEPHEN SOMMERVILLE
DEBS,
CLAIRE CLIFTON

SPECIAL THANKS MUST
ALSO GO TO
MICHAEL DOVER AND
SUSAN HAYNES AT
WEIDENFELD &
NICOLSON:
MICHAEL FOR ALL HIS
DEDICATED INTEREST,
AND SUSAN FOR HER
ENTHUSIASM,
AS WELL AS
TO NIGEL SOPER.
MOST OF ALL,
MY GRATITUDE AND
LOVE GOES TO
JULIET NICOLSON, THE
BEST LITERARY AGENT
ANYONE COULD HAVE,
AND SOMEONE WHO WAS
ALWAYS THERE WITH AN
ENCOURAGING WORD
AND INVALUABLE
ADVICE.

# *B*ibliography

Coats, Alice M, *The Treasury of Flowers* (Phaidon, 1975).

Ewart, Neil - *The Lore of Flowers* (Blandford Press, 1982)

Forshay, Ella M. Foshay, *Art in Bloom* (Phaidon Universe, 1990).

Grigson, Geoffrey, *The Englishman's Flora* (Helicon Publishing Ltd, 1958).

Jarman, Derek, *Derek Jarman's Garden* (Thames and Hudson, 1995).

John, Elton and Taupin, Bernie, *The Complete Lyrics* (Hyperion, 1994).

Lane Fox, Robin, *Vita Sackville-West, The Illustrated Garden Book, Anthology* (Michael Joseph, Ltd, 1986).

Mabey, Richard, *Flora Britannica* (Sinclair-Stevenson, 1996).

McIntyre Anne, *The Complete Floral Healer* (Gaia Books Ltd, 1996).

Milo Ohrbach, Barbara, *Simply Flowers* (Ebury Press, 1993).

Norman, Philip, *Elton – The Definitive Biography* (Hutchinson, 1991).

Perry, Frances, *Flowers of the World* (Hamlyn Publishing Group Ltd, 1972).

Reilly, Ann, *The Rose* (Portland House, 1989).

Sinclair Rohde, Eleanour, *The Story of the Garden* ( ).

Sinclair Rohde, Eleanour, *The Scented Garden* ( ).

Tobler, John, *Elton John - Twenty-five Years in the Charts* (Hamlyn, 1995).

Verey, Rosemary, *The English Country Garden* (BBC Books, 1996).

# Names of flowers and plants used in flower arrangements

agapanthus

alstroemeria

amaryllis

anemone

antirrhinum

camellia

carnation

chinese lantern

chocolate plant

chrysanthemum

copper beech

cotonis

cow parsley

cyclamen

daffodil

dahlia

daisy (michaelmas)

delphinium

eschscholzia 'californica'

eucalyptus

euphorbia

foxglove

fritillary

geranium

gerbera ('Lynx')

  'Dr Who'

  'King'

  'Serena'

ginger

gladiolus

grape hyacinth

honeysuckle (evergreen)

hyacinth

hydrangea

ilex

ivy

jasmine

lilac

lily

  'Arum'

  'Casablanca'

  'La Rêve'

  'Longhi'

  'Peruvian'

  'Stargazer'

lisianthus

majoram

maple

marigold

mimosa

mint

moss

narcissus

orange blossom

orchid

  'Cymbidium'

  'Maggie Wee'

  'Phalaenopsis'

  'Singapore'

peony

phlox

plums

poinsettia

primula

prunus

rhododendron leaf

rose

  Black Tea'

  'Bluebird'

  'Cappucino'

  'Chamilla'

  'Christmas'

  'Climbing Iceberg'

  'Delila'

  'Ecstasy'

  'Emily'

  'Estelle'

  'Gelda Rose'

  'Hollywood'

  'Iceberg'

  'Jacaranda'

  'Leonora'

  'Madame Alfred Carrière'

  'Mountbatten'

  'New Dawn'

  'Nicole'

  'Only Love'

  'Pareo'

  'Profita'

  'Queen Beatrix'

  'Renata'

  'Ravel'

  'Sasha'

  'Souplesse'

  'Sunrise'

  'Unique'

  'Valerie'

rosehip

rose leaf

ranunculus

salvia

salvia 'Argentina'

sandarsonia

scabious

spindleberry

stephanotis

sunflower

sweet pea

tulip

vine leaf

viola 'Adorata'

violacea

waterlily

willow

# $\mathcal{A}$cknowledgements

INTRODUCTION.
'I never gave myself time to stop and smell the roses. Well, now I can stop and I'm going to. I just want to smell a few roses.' ('Jonathan Ross Radio Show', December 1990.)

CHAPTER 1.
' … as if a blue cloud had fallen from the face of heaven, lighting up the darkness of the forest.' (*The Lore of Flowers*, Neil Ewart, Blandford Press, 1982.)

'Bracken refused to acknowledge the child and lost its flower, Ladys Bedstraw welcomed the child and, blossoming at that moment, found its flowers had changed from white to gold.' (*The Englishman's Flora*, Geoffrey Grigson, Helicon Publishing Ltd, Oxford, 1958.)

' … I think I have always been a mummy's boy …' (David Furnish documentary: 'Elton John: Tantrums and Tiaras', 1996.)

CHAPTER 2.
'I grew up with inanimate objects as my friends and I still believe they have feelings. That's why I keep hold of my possessions. I'll look at them and remember when they gave me a bit of happiness.' (Interview with *Playboy Magazine*, 1975.)

' … As we're bobbing up and down, the queen comes up with an equerry and says: "Do you mind if we join you?" Just at that moment the music segues into Bill Haley's 'Rock Around the Clock'. So I am dancing to 'Rock Around the Clock' with the queen of England.' (Interview with Philip Norman, 1992.)

CHAPTER 3.
' … I wanted a house that was comfortable, where people could come and stay, that was full of love and peace. I think that is what this house is about.' (David Furnish documentary.)

'I hoover and dust. I used to love ironing too. It soothed me. Always emptying ashtrays, washing and putting them away.' (Interview with Caroline Coon, Melody Maker, June 1975.)

'As soon as anyone tries to find out about me or to get to know me, I turn off, I'm afraid of getting hurt. I was hurt so much as a kid.' (Interview with Cliff Jahr, *Rolling Stone Magazine*, 1975.)

CHAPTER 4.
'I'm not one for visual things. I don't like doing videos. I don't like my photo being taken. It's probably because of the way I look, the way I think I look and the way I wished I look. I'm not Madonna. I'm not someone who has a very strong visual image, so I don't feel that comfortable.' (Tony Parsons interview as seen in David Furnish's documentary.)

' … I take so much because I never know what to wear and I like to have a choice … '

' … People think you are crazy – I suppose it is crazy but it does keep me sane.'
(Tony Parsons interview as seen in David Furnish's documentary.)

' … I think I'm a good – a great – melody writer. I wish I could write my own lyrics, but I can't.' (Interview with Ian Parker, *The Sunday Times*, December 1996.)

'I actually like working for a living. Of course I feel trapped by it all sometimes, but I love it.' (David Furnish documentary.)

' … Audiences have always been very kind and generous to me. I was always embarrassed by it and I suppose I just didn't trust their affection. I didn't know how to respond or how to accept praise.' (Interview with Ian Parker, *The Sunday Times*, December, 1996.)

'But I have begun to crack the audience thing although I'm still not great with personal compliments. All this stuff about you have to love yourself – that's a hard thing to do.' (David Furnish documentary.)

CHAPTER 5.
'The football club helped me through a really difficult time. It gave me something else to do, rather than be Elton John all the time.'

' … that was bought in the cocaine days. "Get me a tram", she said.' (Interview with Ian Parker, *The Sunday Times*, December 1996.)

CHAPTER 6
'When I announced I was gay in 1976, a lot of radio stations in the US stopped playing my records.' (Interview with Paula Yates on TV programme, 'The Tube'.)

'When it comes to my sexuality, living a lie is not worth it. You only get one attempt on this earth and it is so much better to be yourself. When you do a concert for the foundation it is so much more pleasurable than a normal concert because you know you are raising a lot of money for a really good cause.'

'I've lost quite a few people this year – people I really loved a lot, including Mark, a dear friend who worked for the band and someone whom I've known for seven years. He was only twenty-four and the sweetest boy. Once he got ill he never had another chance. Even though we expected him to die in a couple of weeks, it just shook me. I've really stopped counting all the friends who have died of AIDS this year. I think politicians who say AIDS isn't really a problem, are misinformed. I think they're bigoted and their anger is homophobic. Bigots will be bigots and they will always attack the people they hate the most. So it doesn't surprise me.' (David Furnish documentary.)

Photos of Elton John on page xx courtesy of Rex Features and page xx courtesy of Pictorial Press

# Index